Personal, social and emotional development

■ Planning and Assessment ■ Stepping Stones ■ Early Learning Goals ■ Practical activity ideas

Barbara J Leach

Goals for the Foundation Stage

British Library Cataloguing-in-Publication Data
A catalogue record for this book is available from the British Library.

ISBN 0 439 98349 5

Author
Barbara J Leach

Editor
Lesley Sudlow

Designer
Clare Brewer

Assistant Editor
Victoria Lee

Illustrations
Beccy Blake

Series Designer
Clare Brewer

Cover photography
Derek Cooknell

Text © 2003 Barbara J Leach
© 2003 Scholastic Ltd

Designed using Adobe Pagemaker

Published by Scholastic Ltd,
Villiers House,
Clarendon Avenue,
Leamington Spa,
Warwickshire CV32 5PR

Visit our website at www.scholastic.co.uk
Printed by Proost NV, Belgium

1 2 3 4 5 6 7 8 9 0   3 4 5 6 7 8 9 0 1 2

Acknowledgements
Qualifications and Curriculum Authority for the use of extracts from the QCA/DfEE document *Curriculum Guidance for the Foundation Stage* © 2000 Qualifications and Curriculum Authority.
Every effort has been made to trace copyright holders and the publishers apologise for any inadvertent omissions.

Contents

Personal, social and emotional development

Goals for the Foundation Stage

Personal, social and emotional development

Introduction

This series aims to provide practical activities to support the Early Learning Goals identified by the Qualifications and Curriculum Authority (QCA) and set out in detail in the *Curriculum Guidance for the Foundation Stage*. Each book focuses on one of the six Areas of Learning into which the Foundation Stage is organised and aims to provide ideas for early years practitioners to assist planning, assessment and teaching within the early years curriculum. There are suggested ideas for practical activities to cover the Early Learning Goals and the Stepping Stones leading to those Goals. These ideas can be applied equally well to the documents on pre-school education published for Scotland, Wales and Northern Ireland. The ideas are supported by a range of photocopiable activity sheets, templates and assessment resource sheets that can be used by anyone working with under fives in a variety of different settings.

Personal, social and emotional development

This book concentrates on Personal, social and emotional development and contains a wide range of activity ideas covering all six clusters of the Early Learning Goals: 'dispositions and attitudes', 'self-confidence and self-esteem', 'making relationships', 'behaviour and self-control', 'self-care' and 'sense of community'. Successful personal, social and emotional development forms a crucial part of a young child's life and will determine their ultimate success as a useful and productive member of society when they reach adulthood. It is therefore vital to support children in developing a positive attitude towards both

© JOHN FORTUNATO/SODA

themselves and others, by providing pleasurable experiences that will further this development.

Personal, social and emotional development is essentially cross-curricular since children need to learn to share equipment, space and adult time and attention throughout their day, both in the setting and elsewhere. It is also the foundation for all past, present and future learning and it is important to ensure that it is given due prominence when planning activities so that the children are given ample opportunity to form positive relationships, develop a high self-esteem and gain the confidence to take care of themselves in a supportive environment. The activities contained in this book aim to provide those opportunities in an interesting and pleasurable way, thus fostering a lifelong love of learning.

Aspects of learning

This book will assist early years practitioners to offer a wide range of such opportunities, with each chapter covering one of the six aspects of learning within Personal, social and emotional development. In Chapter 1 there are activities to cover each of the ten Stepping Stones leading to the three Early Learning Goals within the 'dispositions and attitudes' cluster, ranging from colour-mixing and porridge-making activities to foster the children's sense of curiosity, to a hiding and finding game to encourage them to take risks and explore within the environment. Similarly, from Chapter 2 to Chapter 6, at least one activity is suggested for every Stepping Stone within each aspect of learning, providing activities such as making Eid cards and Divali candles, to develop a sense of self as a member of different communities, as well as singing and miming games to promote a positive self-image.

Stepping Stones

Children very rarely develop physically, emotionally or intellectually at an even rate and the Stepping Stones set out in the *Curriculum Guidance for the Foundation Stage* are not age-related. However, progression is shown throughout this stage by the use of three coloured bands of steps leading to each cluster of Early Learning Goals. This book is organised to provide a progression of ideas within each aspect of learning contained in each chapter. The activities are grouped to cover specific Early Learning Goals and progress through each band of Stepping Stones to achieve these, for example, in Chapter 2 there are three distinct Goals contained within the 'self-confidence and self-esteem' cluster.

The first of these Goals 'Respond to significant experiences, showing a range of feelings when appropriate' is covered by four activities: one covering a Stepping Stone within the first colour band, two within the

© KEN KARP/SODA

second, and one within the third. The second Goal 'Have a developing awareness of their own needs, views and feelings and be sensitive to the needs, views and feelings of others' is covered by three activities: two from the second coloured band of Stepping Stones, and one from the third. The final Goal within this aspect of learning 'Have a developing respect for their own cultures and beliefs and those of other people' is also covered by three activities: one from the second coloured band and two from the third.

© KEN KARP/SODA

How to use this book

This book can be utilised in a number of different ways. Each activity is designed so that it can be used as a single, stand-alone activity to support one particular aspect of personal, social and emotional development. It is therefore possible to dip in and out of the book to find an activity to suit certain children, at a particular stage of learning, at any time.

The book is not designed to be worked through systematically, however it does contain a broad range of ideas using a variety of materials and equipment normally found in early years settings and covers a wide range of play areas including outdoor play, sand and construction toys, role-play, art and craft, cookery, music and physical activities. It could therefore provide a sound basis for developing a broad and well-balanced personal, social and emotional development programme.

There are also further suggestions for adapting the ideas to support the learning of younger or less able children or extending the ideas for use with older or more able children.

At the end of each activity there are 'More ideas' to help achieve the same Early Learning Goal.

Photocopiable sheets

To further support the children's learning there are a number of photocopiable resource sheets primarily designed to be used for a particular activity, but which can also be used in a number of other ways. For example, the 'This is me' photocopiable sheet used alongside the 'Look at me' activity on page 56 of Chapter 4, could also be used as a colouring sheet or be copied on to card to make a stick puppet. Another idea would be to enlarge it and use it with labels to identify and name external body parts, or copy it on to thick card and cut it up to make a jigsaw puzzle.

There are also photocopiable templates that could be adapted, for example, the 'Dreidel cube' photocopiable sheet on page 95 could be changed to make a customised dice or enlarged for the children to make their own dice or alphabet or building cubes.

Curriculum links

Although the Foundation Stage Curriculum is divided into six distinct Areas of Learning, it is intended to provide an integrated education for children in their early years. The more links that can be made across the whole curriculum, the deeper the understanding a child will gain. Everyone uses a variety of mathematical, linguistic, social, creative and physical skills throughout the day, and no particular subject can, or should be, taught or learned in isolation. This is particularly true of Personal, social and emotional development. It underpins everything that we do throughout our lives, for example, how we relate to others, our attitudes to learning, our ability to concentrate and persist at difficult tasks and how we feel about ourselves, are all essential aspects of education. It is therefore important that children are constantly encouraged and given the opportunity to develop these skills.

At the end of each activity in this book there is an 'Other curriculum areas' section for cross-curricular links to assist practitioners to achieve the same Stepping Stone or Early Learning Goal in a different Area of Learning, thus providing an integrated and sound basis for each child's personal development. These are identified in the shortened form of PSED (Personal, social and emotional development), CLL (Communication, language and literacy), MD (Mathematical development), KUW (Knowledge and understanding of the world), PD (Physical development) and CD (Creative development) to match the six Areas of Learning.

Home links

The children's first educators are their parents and it is essential that an effective partnership is developed with them right from the start. It is sometimes difficult to make time in a busy working day to ensure that there is a constant two-way flow of information and understanding, but this is essential if the children are to be educated to the very best level. There is a 'Home links' section at the end of each activity to assist the practitioner to keep the lines of communication open between the setting and home in a variety of informal ways.

Personal, social and emotional development

Planning

Effective and efficient planning is an important part of early years practitioners' work. It helps to ensure that a variety of activities and experiences are offered over a period of time, therefore creating a lively, exciting and challenging learning environment for all the children in the setting, from the beginning to the end of the Foundation Stage. This chapter contains guidance for all early years practitioners to  help with planning so that they are able to provide progression throughout the Foundation Stage in the area of Personal, social and emotional development.

Planning for a progression of ideas

As mentioned in the 'Introduction' on page 5, the activities within this book are directly linked to the *Curriculum Guidance for the Foundation Stage* and cover all six aspects of learning within the Personal, social and emotional development area. This particular Area of Learning is extremely important at all times and certain aspects of development, such as learning how to share and take turns (making relationships), or showing care and concern for the environment (behaviour and self-control), will of course be an integral part of daily life within the setting across the entire curriculum. However, practitioners may wish to pay the area particular attention at certain times, for example, when settling in new arrivals or when preparing the children for a day trip to a place of interest or moving on to a different setting. It will be important at times to offer particular activities to children to provide the necessary opportunities for them to develop certain skills or attitudes, such as how to relate to others and make attachments to members of their group (making relationships), or learning to sit quietly when appropriate (dispositions and attitudes).

Each chapter in this book deals with a different aspect of learning in order to facilitate finding particular activities to cover specific Stepping Stones appropriate at various stages of the Foundation Stage. This in turn will enable your planning to reflect the extra prominence given to Personal, social and emotional development at various times throughout the Foundation Stage.

Personal, social and emotional development

Equal opportunities

Children that attend early years settings come from a rich variety of backgrounds and with a broad range of previous experiences and skills. It is important, therefore, that practitioners plan to ensure that every child in their care should feel welcome in the group and that their thoughts and ideas are valued and respected from the beginning. The *Curriculum Guidance for the Foundation Stage* (QCA) contains information and advice about how to plan for the diverse needs of children (see pages 17, 18 and 19 of the document) so that they are able to reach their full potential. Most children should achieve the Early Learning Goals and some will progress beyond this by the end of the Foundation Stage, but it is important that appropriately challenging learning opportunities are planned and provided to enable all children to achieve as fully as possible whatever their starting-point.

Practitioners should plan to meet the needs of children from either gender, children with special educational needs, more able children, children from different ethnic backgrounds such as travellers, asylum seekers and refugees, children from all religious, social and cultural backgrounds, children from various linguistic backgrounds and children with disabilities. It is important that practitioners are fully aware of the content of the various Acts that cover the requirements of equal opportunities. These are the Sex Discrimination Act (1975), the Race Relations Act (1976) and the Disability Discrimination Act (1995). Planning should also take into account the requirements of the revised SEN *Code of Practice* (2002).

The activities within this book aim to meet the requirements set out in these documents and should therefore be suitable for use with any child in any setting, though some may need adapting slightly to suit certain conditions. For example, 'Footprints' on page 60 may require specialist equipment such as a long-handled sponge in order to include a wheelchair-bound child in this activity. Further guidance with regard to planning for children with special educational needs or disabilities is given on page 5 of *Planning for Learning in the Foundation Stage* (QCA). The document (reference QCA/01/799) is available free of charge from QCA Publications, tel: 01787 884444 or e-mail: qca@prolog.uk.com

The document provides essential and useful advice regarding the new duties brought in by the SEN and Disability Act (2001) which will enable the Disability Discrimination Act to be extended in September 2002 to cover education.

Long-term planning

Long-term plans should be based on the six Areas of Learning identified by QCA and should provide an overview of the various learning opportunities that will be offered to children in a setting over a period of time. The plans will, of course, be influenced by conditions within that setting regarding interior and exterior building design and layout, available facilities, staffing levels and other environmental factors, but ultimately they will aim to offer as broad and balanced a curriculum as possible. Long-term plans need not dictate how or when particular opportunities are offered as this could make them unduly restrictive, when in fact they should be sufficiently flexible to allow staff to introduce specific activities according to the developing needs of the children at any one time. A suitable long-term plan might include an indication of:

■ the Stepping Stones that you intend to cover in each of the six areas during various periods of time

■ cross-curricular themes that you intend to use to link the various learning and teaching aspects of the different areas

■ special events that you are planning in order to enhance the curriculum.

You should also ensure that the plan covers all aspects of learning within all six Areas of Learning, and that it provides opportunities to revisit all of those aspects frequently and on a regular basis. *Planning for Learning in the Foundation Stage* (QCA) contains a useful numbered list on page 20 of all areas and aspects of learning for the Foundation Stage. An example of a long-term plan is shown on page 11 of the document.

Medium-term planning

Some practitioners find drawing up medium-term plans to be helpful, though many will find that long-term and short-term plans are sufficient for their purposes. Medium-term plans bridge the gap between the overview outlined in the long-term plan and the detail contained in the

Personal, social and emotional development

short-term plans. They should expand upon the teaching and learning intentions outlined in the long-term plan and identify the activities that will be offered in order to meet those intentions. Medium-term plans should also include information regarding the organisation and teaching strategies that will be employed, the groupings and resources that will be used and the assessment opportunities that will be presented. They generally cover a period of between six and eight weeks and often use a separate grid for each Area of Learning.

Short-term planning

Short-term plans are derived from long-term plans and further expand upon the details in any medium-term plans that might be used. They contain the day-to-day detail of how things are going to be carried out, the adjustments that are going to be made to cater for children with different needs, how links can be made between the various Areas of Learning and an assessment of the learning that has taken place. They are generally drawn up on a day-to-day or weekly basis and should take into account the changing needs, circumstances or conditions within the setting. Short-term plans must be clear, concise and easy to complete and will often include specific details such as the vocabulary that will be used during a particular activity. They should also include information regarding the role of the adult – including parent helpers – and should cover all six Areas of Learning. Examples of short-term plans are shown in the document *Planning for Learning in the Foundation stage* (QCA).

Organisation

Every setting is uniquely different and each has its own set of problems, but whatever the practical difficulties are, the role of the adult within every setting remains the same – to support the children's learning and to further their progress in all areas of development and learning. This underpins everything that is undertaken within the setting and should remain at the forefront of everyone's mind.

© JAMES LEVIN/SODA

Practitioners working alone may find it useful to meet with others to share ideas and discuss any particular organisational problems that they may be experiencing. Those working in a team will need to have a clear idea of their own roles and responsibilities within that team in order to provide the children with a secure, stable and stimulating environment, offering an appropriately broad and balanced curriculum.

There are many diverse ways to organise an early years environment, but all rely on structure and routine. It is essential to establish a pattern for the day to enable the children in your care to feel confident and secure. It is important that all adults within the setting work together to plan suitable routines for the children's arrival and departure so that they are clear in their own minds about the procedure and can help and reassure any children – or indeed carers – who may be unsure what to do.

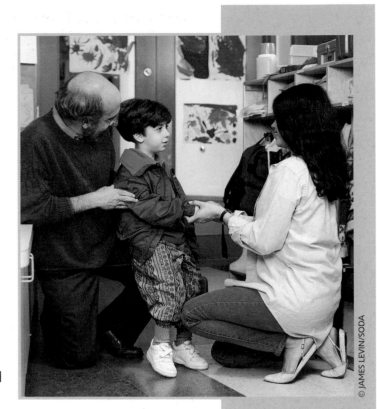

It is also of great significance to ensure that all adults within the setting are aware of, and fully understand, any particular 'house rules' that you may have, for example, about the children bringing snacks or toys from home. Planning regular meetings to discuss organisational matters can be extremely useful and can prevent any misunderstandings or misconceptions getting out of hand.

It is often useful to assign a key worker to each child, particularly in larger settings, as this gives both the child and the carer a point of contact and helps to keep the line of communication open between home and setting. Organising the children into colour groups and giving them identifying name badges can also be useful ways to give the children a sense of belonging. You may also wish to consider displaying a pictorial timetable to familiarise the children with the basic pattern of the day (see 'Here I am' on page 30) so that they can anticipate what is going to happen when.

An essential element in the provision of a good environment for learning is the resources, and practitioners should plan to check and replace these regularly to keep them in good repair, to ensure that they are still appropriate to the needs of the children and that they remain attractive and safe to use.

Setting up a suitable play environment

Practitioners play a crucial role in securing a child's personal, social and emotional development. They are the role models for the children, and the way they speak and behave will be reflected in the way that the children learn to respond to people and events around them. It is practitioners who organise the children's environment and provide the resources for their play, and it is they who support and extend their play and learning experiences. The most important resource in any setting is the practitioner, so it is essential that all adults working with young children are fully conversant with the *Curriculum Guidance for the Foundation Stage* (QCA) and are able to act as the positive role models that young children need.

Personal, social and emotional development takes place constantly, throughout every day, in every area of children's lives. They are being continuously bombarded with new experiences – negative as well as positive – new situations and new faces, and they must try to make sense of it all. It is therefore important that we feelings of confidence and self-worth are fostered in the children in the setting to help them develop a positive disposition to life and learning.

This Area of Learning can be covered in play areas from sand and water activities, through to art and craft activities and natural discovery. There are specific activities included within this book that enable practitioners to cover the Personal, social and emotional curriculum requirements in all those areas:

■ Sand play – 'Tunnel around' on page 52 provides an opportunity for the children to show confidence and the ability to stand up for themselves while constructing tunnels of every shape and size.

■ Water play – 'Rainy-day fun' on page 63 allows the children the chance to play with water straight from the skies after tackling the developmentally appropriate task of getting themselves suitably dressed to go out in the rain.

■ Role-play – 'Ding-ding – we're off!' on page 46 encourages the children to relate and make attachments to members of their group while they take turns to drive a 'bus' to unknown destinations.

■ Outdoor environment – 'Dig it up' on page 51 offers the children the chance to get their hands dirty during gardening while they learn how to show care and concern for living things and the environment.

■ Art and craft – 'Fabulous fish' on page 65 helps to give the children a sense of pride in their own achievement as they exercise their artistic talents.

■ Natural discovery – 'Who lives here?' on page 55 allows the children to explore the world around them showing due care and concern for living things and the environment.

■ Construction – 'Hmm! I wonder...' on page 64 offers the children a chance to test their building skills as they show a willingness to tackle problems and enjoy self-chosen challenges.

■ Malleable materials – 'Look what I've made' on page 67 encourage the children to take initiatives and manage developmentally appropriate tasks as they mould play dough into ever-changing shapes.

© JOHN FORTUNATO/SODA

Assessment

The importance of assessment

Assessment plays a crucial role in helping early years practitioners to monitor and understand children's learning and thus identify ways to support and extend that learning. Ongoing assessments will help to inform their planning and enable them to provide a rich and stimulating curriculum for all the children in their care – whatever their level of development. Observation is a constant and integral part of working with young children and it has been noted by Ofsted that:

'Careful assessments based on regular observations are the key elements in ensuring that the curriculum for the under fives is based on the needs of the pupils and provides continuity and progression'.

It is essential that early assessments of children's learning should focus on what they can do, rather than what they cannot do, in order to give a sound starting-point for further development. The views of parents and carers should be sought and taken into account when a child first enters a setting, along with views and information from any other professional that has been involved with the child, such as medical personnel, a speech therapist, social worker and so on, and subsequently has some knowledge and understanding of their needs and abilities.

Regular assessment

Careful and regular assessment also enables practitioners to evaluate the learning that has taken place so far and allows them to identify any individual problems as they arise, so that they may be dealt with, perhaps by adapting or extending the activities or equipment that they provide, or calling in an outside agency for specialist advice in order to cater for the diverse needs of the individual children in their care.

Detailed assessment

Detailed observations and assessment can also provide insight into the way that a child learns and can help to identify any gaps in their learning that may be hindering progress. This allows the matter to be addressed and dealt with in a systematic and practical way, and helps to move the child's learning forward. There may also be children with special educational needs or disabilities within a setting and it is important that they are identified as early as possible in order to provide them with the necessary resources, such as specialist teaching, adapted equipment or adult support, for the activities undertaken. This is particularly important

Personal, social and emotional development

in the area of Personal, social and emotional development since it is essential that every child should have the opportunity to become a valued member of a group, in order to build a strong self-image and self-esteem, and has been provided with a sound basis for future learning and personal development.

Detailed and systematic assessments are also necessary to establish whether a child is making steady progress across all the Areas of Learning. Any areas of weakness can then be targeted and become the focus of attention for a short period so that specific reasons for that weakness can be identified and addressed. Extra support, or more opportunities for learning in that area, will be needed to overcome, or at least minimise, the weakness. This may, in turn, help to avoid further learning difficulties in the future.

Assessment, therefore, should be part of a practitioner's daily practice and through it they should aim to observe and evaluate the children's learning so that they can act upon this information to provide the children with the best possible start on their road to life-long learning.

Recommended methods of assessment

Informal assessments

During every session, early years practitioners are continually making informal assessments about the children as they observe, talk and listen to them while they go about their activities. These assessments can often be used to amend or adjust activities that are in progress, in order to extend the learning of older or more able children, or to support the learning of younger or less able children, without altering the essential essence of that activity.

The activities within this book each contain suggestions for such support and extension work should you require them. Informal assessments can also be used to amend activities planned for the future, in order to cater for the changing needs of children within the group. Many practitioners will find it useful to have a small notepad and pen

close at hand, so that jottings can be made to ensure that such assessments and evaluations are not forgotten in the course of a busy day. These notes can then form the basis of daily or weekly planning sessions when all adults working within the setting can get together to discuss and appraise the activities and evaluate the learning that has taken place, in order to plan the next steps, thus ensuring continuity and progression.

Other evidence of learning may be collected informally, by way of photographs of the children working or playing together, the models or structures that they have built, their marks on paper, audio recordings of their conversations or comments, and verbatim reports of their explanations about activities that they have done.

Personal, social and emotional development

Formal assessments

Although informal observations and assessments are extremely important, there is also a place for more formal, planned assessments and observations, in order to ascertain whether children are progressing in all Areas across the curriculum and to ensure that their needs are being identified correctly and are addressed.

© JAMES LEVIN/SODA

It is crucial, when making a formal observation, that practitioners have a particular focus in mind for that observation and that they record what the child or children are actually doing, without trying to interpret or make judgements about their behaviour. Similarly when recording what a child is saying, practitioners should ensure that they use the child's actual words, not their interpretation of them. In this way, the data that is collected will be an accurate record of events and can be used to evaluate the activity and to decide upon future action to support or extend learning.

A simple 'Observation record sheet' is provided on page 82. It contains an Evaluation/support/extension column that can be completed after the observation and in consultation with co-workers, if desired. The sheet can be used in many different situations as well as for any activity and, if completed regularly, could provide useful information for planning purposes. It could also be used to monitor the behaviour of a particular child, or group of children, who may be causing concern.

Areas of Learning

It is important to build up a number of observations across all the Areas of Learning. Although focuses of attention may differ for each Area, there are certain things that are common to all the Areas that may prove to be useful starting-points for regular observations, for example, the child's level and span of concentration, their ability to practise and extend their skills, their competence to solve practical problems, their willingness to persevere in the face of difficulty and their ability to initiate ideas. Focuses for observations and assessments that are relevant to Personal, social and emotional development can be set with direct reference to the Stepping Stones for this Area of Learning, thus providing the necessary cross-reference to planning.

While the Stepping Stones contained in the *Curriculum Guidance for the Foundation Stage* (QCA) may not be a totally exhaustive list of personal skills, they do provide a useful framework for the progression of such skills from the beginning to the end of the Foundation Stage. They can be used to monitor the development of children in a systematic way across the entire early years curriculum.

Foundation Stage Profile

In January 2003, the Qualifications and Curriculum Authority introduced a new assessment document for early years practitioners working within the Foundation Stage. The *Foundation Stage Profile* provides a 12-page document to be completed for each child throughout the Foundation Stage. Within it the curriculum is broken down to provide assessment for all six Areas of Learning. For Personal, social and emotional development there are 27 'targets'.

Practitioners will be expected to use their usual techniques of observation and occasional note-taking to gather evidence of children's skills and abilities.

Using this book for assessment

The photocopiable assessment sheets on pages 79 to 81 are designed to provide a means of recording the children's personal progress throughout the Foundation Stage. The sheets provide details of the Early Learning Goals that the children need to achieve by the end of this stage. Space has been provided on each sheet for you to make notes and observations about individual children's progress.

Allow the children plenty of settling-in time to your setting before you make a formal assessment. Half way through the time that the child will be at your setting, follow up the first assessment with a second record of achievement, then make a final assessment at the end of the child's learning period.

© JOHN FORTUNATO/SODA

Remember to include any special information about individual children. It may also be worth recording how frequent their grasp of a certain skill is, as some children remember how to complete a task one day and appear to have lost the very same skill another! Also include the level of adult support needed to achieve a certain objective.

Keep the sheets to hand on to the children's next setting, or for discussion with parents, carers and other adults that work with the children. However, while written plans and records of achievement are necessary, their preparation and completion should not take up an undue amount of your time.

This chapter provides opportunities for the children to experience a variety of exciting activities. The ideas suggest play-based activities that will help the children to foster a love of learning, encourage a sense of curiosity and appeal to their exploratory instincts.

Multicoloured dough

What to do

■ Give each child a small ball of play dough and talk together about its colour and texture.

■ Invite each child to make a small indentation in the top of their play dough while you fill an eye dropper with some paint.

■ Ask the children what they think will happen if you put a few drops of paint in the dent in the play dough then squeeze it.

■ Add the paint and let the children work it into the dough and encourage them to say whether their predictions were correct.

■ Look at the balls of dough, compare them and talk about the colour distribution in each one.

■ Repeat the activity with new dough and different colours. Let the children use the eye droppers and encourage them to talk about what they are doing and what they can see happening.

■ Put the eye droppers to one side and invite each child to select two coloured balls of dough and ask them to predict what will happen if they mix them together.

■ Let the children mix the play dough together and say whether their predictions were correct.

■ Give the children time to experiment freely with the paints and dough.

■ Use different-coloured play dough rather than eye droppers and paint with younger children.

■ Encourage older children to record the activity pictorially.

More ideas

■ Bury small items such as marbles, shiny buttons or new pennies in dry sand and let the children unearth the 'treasure' using sieves or colanders.

■ Hold familiar objects up behind a back-lit screen and invite the children to guess what they are from their shadows.

Other curriculum areas

KUW Take the children on a walk and look for creatures under logs and stones. Find out more about them in books when you get back to the setting.

MD Gift wrap geometrically-shaped everyday objects, such as groceries, and let the children handle them, talk about how they feel and guess what is inside.

Stepping Stone
Show curiosity.

Early Learning Goal
Continue to be interested, excited and motivated to learn.

Group size
Four to six children.

What you need
Uncoloured play dough; paint; eye droppers.

Home links
Ask parents and carers to play 'Describe and guess' games with their children at home to develop their descriptive vocabulary and foster a sense of excitement about learning.

Whose box is it?

Stepping Stone
Have a strong exploratory impulse.

Early Learning Goal
Continue to be interested, excited and motivated to learn.

Group size
Up to ten children.

What you need
A set of colourfully-decorated boxes that fit inside each other; interesting object to put into the smallest box such as a magic wand or a clown's red nose.

What to do
■ Pack the boxes one inside the other with the 'treasure' inside.
■ Gather the children and tell them that you have found something very interesting.
■ Show them the box and encourage them to guess who it might have belonged to and what might be inside, for example, a magician's box perhaps, containing a wand or spell, or a clown's box containing a red nose or braces.

■ Slowly remove the lid and excitedly disclose the second box.
■ Repeat the process, maintaining interest and excitement as each subsequent box is revealed by encouraging the children to imagine all sorts of potential owners and contents until finally the object inside is revealed.
■ Use just three or four boxes with younger children and let them take turns to remove the lid each time.
■ Play the game a second time with older children and put a clue to the enclosed object in each box to help them guess what it might be.

More ideas
■ Put an object in a cloth bag and let the children feel it and guess what it is before they see it.
■ Bring in unfamiliar objects and encourage the children to handle them and ask questions about them in order to guess what they are.
■ Provide interesting sand- and water-play equipment such as pumps, siphons and mechanical scoops for the children to explore.

Home links
Ask parents and carers to let you have any old items such as mechanical clocks or keys and locks for the children to investigate and take apart.

Other curriculum areas
KUW Let the children freely investigate items, such as mirrors or magnets.
CD Encourage the children to mix their own paints and give them opportunities to explore the colours and textures of the paints
CLL Provide lift-the-tab books for the children to handle and explore.

Water play

What to do

■ Gather the group around the tray and tell them that it is empty because you cannot think of what to put in it.

■ Ask the children if they would like warm or cold water? Do they want it coloured or clear, bubbly or plain?

■ Continue to ask questions and encourage careful thought as you gather ideas and resources.

■ If too many resources are being suggested, ask the children to think about what will happen if the tray is too crowded, then help them to decide which items to use now and which to put aside for future use.

■ Let the children help you to set up the resources, for example, by adding the cold water while you add the hot, or fetching items from accessible cupboards or shelves.

■ Help younger children to decide what to use in the water tray by providing suitable equipment that is visibly accessible.

■ Invite older children to think of more unusual items that might be suitable to use in the water tray, such as plastic construction bricks or play people, balancing pans and Plasticine to make boats.

More ideas

■ When you change the function of the role-play area, encourage the children to help with the selection and arrangement of resources.

■ Provide the children with a selection of resources and ask them for ideas about how they could be utilised. Help the children to carry out some of their ideas.

Other curriculum areas

CD	Store different types of dressing-up clothes in different boxes and let the children select a box themselves.
PD	Challenge the children to build their own fitness trails using planks, steps, boxes and tubes.
MD	Encourage the children to make up their own counting, adding or subtracting games using dice or dominoes.

Stepping Stone
Show increasing independence in selecting and carrying out activities.

Early Learning Goal
Continue to be interested, excited and motivated to learn.

■

Group size
Up to six children.

■

What you need
An empty water tray; resources requested by the children!

Home links
When a child acquires a new skill such as tying shoelaces or cutting along a line, celebrate this by praising them in front of their parent or carer at home time and encourage them to practise it further at home.

Personal, social and emotional development

Porridge pot

Stepping Stone
Show curiosity.

Early Learning Goal
Be confident to try new activities, initiate ideas and speak in a familiar group.

Group size
Up to six children.

What you need
Instant porridge; mixing bowl; warm milk; cold milk; salt; sugar; raisins; water; jam; plenty of small dishes or clean yoghurt pots; teaspoons.

Preparation
Check for any food allergies and dietary requirements.

What to do
■ Gather the children together and invite them to watch as you make a bowl of instant porridge, gradually stirring in warm milk to make it smooth and creamy.

■ Give each child a dish, spoon and small amount of porridge.

■ Invite the children to taste the porridge. Encourage them to describe its flavour and texture, and to say why they like or dislike it.

■ Make up a second bowl of porridge, this time pouring in cold milk and not stirring it.

■ Again, give each child a dish, spoon and small amount of porridge. What do the children think of this porridge?

■ Spend a few minutes recalling and comparing how the porridges were made before inviting a child to make another bowl of porridge.

■ Show the child the available ingredients and help them to make the porridge to their own recipe, then encourage the rest of the group to taste and talk about it.

■ Repeat until each child has had a turn at making some porridge.

■ Encourage younger children to pretend to be Goldilocks as they taste and talk about the porridge.

■ Help older children to make a chart to show how many children liked the different bowls of porridge.

More ideas
■ Invite local artists or craftspeople to demonstrate their particular skill. Encourage the children to ask questions and maybe have a go themselves.

■ Provide opportunities for the children to demonstrate to each other how to make play dough or mix paints.

Home links
Ask the children to bring a favourite game from home to show to the other children and explain or demonstrate how to play it.

Other curriculum areas
PD　Play games where the children take turns to be the leader.

CLL　Invite each child to select a favourite story-book and to talk to the rest of the group about it.

What is it?

What to do

■ Put some cooked spaghetti into the washing-up bowl and place the bowl inside the feely box.

■ Gather the children around the box and tell them that there is something interesting inside. Invite two children to put their hands through the holes and feel inside the box.

■ Ask 'What does it feel like?', 'Do you like it?', 'What do you think it might be?'.

■ Invite the next pair of children to have a turn and repeat until everyone has felt inside the box.

■ Open the box and reveal its contents.

■ Put the spaghetti to one side and, out of sight of the children, pour rice into the washing-up bowl and place it inside the box.

■ Invite the second pair of children to be first this time and proceed with the activity as before.

■ Repeat the activity with the pasta, then the jelly, each time letting a different pair of children feel the items first. Encourage them to tell the rest of the group as much as possible about what they can feel.

■ Invite younger children to use just the open bowl and encourage them to explore and talk about how the different items feel.

■ Challenge older children by using a mixture of similar items, such as buttons, coins and counters, and ask them to describe the differences.

More ideas

■ Let the children use the leftover spaghetti to make pictures on black paper (the starch in the spaghetti will make it cling to the paper as it dries).

■ Invite the children to dangle spaghetti strands over branches of bushes outside so that birds can feed from it.

Other curriculum areas

MD Use the feely box to play counting, shape-matching and size-comparison games.

CLL Place some everyday objects inside the feely box and challenge the children to try to find something beginning with 's' or 'c'.

PD Put beads and string in the box and challenge the children to thread them together without looking.

Personal, social and emotional development

Let's make butterflies

What to do

■ Put the materials in the middle of the table and invite the children to suggest how you could use them.

■ Let each child tell you their idea and repeat it to ensure that the whole group has heard.

■ Go through the ideas again, for example, 'Carly thinks we could make beautiful crowns; Kai suggested beautiful butterflies; Echo said we could make animal masks. What a lot of wonderful ideas!'.

■ Invite the children to try to make the items using either their own or someone else's idea.

■ Encourage the children to talk about what they are doing as they work and to ask each other for help, if necessary.

■ If a child gets really stuck, stop the group for a few moments to discuss the problem and help to solve it.

■ When each child has finished an item, ask them if they are happy with it or whether they think it could be improved in any way before finally displaying it for everyone to see.

■ Help younger children by holding glued surfaces together while they dry, or cutting out difficult shapes that they might need such as stars or eye holes.

■ Encourage older children to think about their creation before they start cutting and sticking, and to try to organise their own work space.

More ideas

■ Make this activity a regular feature of your sessions, each time providing a slightly different set of materials.

■ Provide plenty of opportunities for the children to personalise their work by selecting their own materials even during more structured adult-led activities.

Other curriculum areas

MD Encourage the children to record counting activities in their own way before introducing more formal methods.

CD Let the children experiment with recyclable materials, glue and sticky tape to discover for themselves the most successful way to join various surfaces together.

Personal, social and emotional development

Find the number

What to do
■ Give each child and yourself a card and a pen.
■ Explain to the children that you are going to play a game called 'Bingo', and that the object of the game is to cross out all the numbers on their board.
■ Demonstrate by rolling the dice, counting the dots, finding the appropriate number and crossing it out on your card.
■ Invite a child to roll the dice to start the game.
■ As the children take turns to roll the dice and find their number, encourage them to ask the child sat next to them for help, if necessary.
■ Carry on playing until everyone has finished.
■ Shorten the game for younger children by letting everyone find and cross out the number each time that the dice is rolled, not just when it is their turn.
■ Let older children share one board between two and encourage them to think of ways that they can work together so that they both play an equal share of the game.

More ideas
■ Encourage the children to play interactive circle games such as 'In and Out the Dusty Bluebells' or 'The Hokey Cokey'.
■ Invite the children to play games in pairs in which one child wears a blindfold and the other verbally supports and encourages them to complete a task, for example, posting shapes in a box or finding a particular shape.

Other curriculum areas
CD Use large sheets of paper and encourage the children to paint or draw in pairs.
CLL Read a familiar story to the children and incorporate mistakes for the children to spot to encourage their aural and visual concentration.
PD Demonstrate to the children how to work together to carry large or awkward equipment, such as tables or crash mats.

Let's act it out

Stepping Stone
Display high levels of involvement in activities.

Early Learning Goal
Maintain attention, concentrate, and sit quietly when appropriate.

Group size
Whole group.

What you need
A story-book with more than one speaking character in it, for example, *Goldilocks and the Three Bears*, *The Three Little Pigs* or *Little Red Riding Hood* (*First Favourite Tales* series, Ladybird Books).

What to do

■ Read the story to the children, emphasising the words that are spoken by the characters.
■ Tell the children that you are going to read the story again, but this time you would like them to help you with some of the words.
■ Divide the children into appropriate groups to suit the number

of speaking characters in the story, for example, three for 'Goldilocks'. Make sure that each group knows which character they are going to be.
■ Read the story again, indicating to each group as their particular character is mentioned.
■ As you read the words spoken by each character, help the relevant children to say those words aloud together.
■ Encourage the children to use facial expressions and intonation to help them get into character.
■ Work with just three or four younger children and say all the spoken parts together as a group.
■ Make sure that you have plenty of space for older children and invite them to stand up when it is their turn to speak and use appropriate movements and gestures to accompany their words.

More ideas

■ Let the children play parachute games to develop group awareness and encourage active involvement.
■ Introduce the children to a wide range of action rhymes and songs.

Other curriculum areas

KUW Create a digging patch outside. Alternatively, use large tubs if you do not have a garden. Provide gloves, tools and wheelbarrows and encourage the children to become involved.

CD Set aside a music corner and encourage the children to make their own instruments or sound makers to add to your collection. Let them demonstrate to their friends how to use them.

Home links
Give each child a copy of the 'Tell a story' photocopiable sheet on page 84 to take home. Ask parents and carers to help their children to cut out the pictures and use them to tell the story of 'Goldilocks and the Three Bears'.

Model it

What to do

■ Spend some time looking at the craft books and gathering ideas with the children.

■ Show the children the materials that are available and invite them to make their own model.

■ If the children are unsure what to make, suggest that they sort through some of the materials to get some ideas.

■ As the children work, be ready to help with practical problems and give them encouragement.

■ If a child begins to lose interest, talk to them about their model to hold their attention a little longer.

■ When a child decides that they have finished their model, help them to think whether they could improve it in any way, perhaps by painting it.

■ If the child does not want to carry on with their model, suggest that they do something else for a while and return later to carry on.

■ Give younger children plenty of attention and encouragement to prolong their interest when making their model.

■ Put aside older children's models and invite them to return to them with renewed enthusiasm during the next session.

More ideas

■ Work together as a group and make a large papier mâché model over several sessions.

■ Use different sand-timers to encourage the children to continue at an activity for gradually longer periods of time.

Other curriculum areas

MD Challenge the children to make the longest paper chain that they can and help them to count the links. Repeat the activity during subsequent sessions to see if they can make each chain longer than the one before.

CLL Gradually increase the length of story-books that you share with the children and read a long one, such as 'Thumbelina' or 'Pinnochio', to sustain the children's interest over several sessions.

Stepping Stone
Persist for extended periods of time at an activity of their choosing.

Early Learning Goal
Maintain attention, concentrate and sit quietly when appropriate.

Group size
Up to eight children.

What you need
Craft books; selection of recyclable materials; scissors; glue; sticky tape; pens; paint; art and craft materials; clothes pegs (for holding glued surfaces together while they dry).

Home links
Hold a sponsored silence to encourage the children to practise sitting quietly and ask parents and carers to sponsor them.

Find the bear

Stepping Stone
Take risks and explore within the environment.

Early Learning Goal
Maintain attention, concentrate, and sit quietly when appropriate.

Group size
Whole group.

What you need
Five or six small items such as a toy car, bead, small-world person, pencil sharpener, model dinosaur, building block and so on; tiny bear; six or seven plastic beakers.

Home links
Encourage parents and carers to let their children know that it is all right to fail or make mistakes, and that even adults do it sometimes, but that we should all try to think before acting.

What to do
■ Gather the children together and explain that you are going to play a game called 'Find the bear'.
■ Show the children the tiny bear, put it on to the table and place a beaker over it.
■ Look at the other items and place a beaker over each one.
■ Ask the children, 'Where is the bear?'.

■ Now tell the children that that was too easy, so you are going to make it more difficult.
■ Invite a child to play first.
■ Ask the child to look away from the beakers while you muddle them all up, putting the bear under a different beaker.
■ Tell the other children that if the child does not find the bear, they should shout, 'That's not the bear!', but if the child does find the bear, they should shout, 'He/She's found the bear!'.
■ Show the child the beakers and invite them to choose a beaker to lift.
■ As each beaker is lifted, the rest of the children should shout a response until finally the bear is found.
■ Congratulate the child that has found the bear and ask them to choose another child to play next.
■ Play the game in a very small group with younger children.
■ Allow older children just three attempts to find the bear before passing their turn to someone else.

More ideas
■ Give the children plenty of independence by having resources easily accessible and encourage them to pour their own squash or mop up their messes.
■ Reposition equipment regularly and introduce new resources to foster the children's exploratory instincts.

Other curriculum areas
KUW Encourage the children to explore and experiment by providing magnets alongside metallic and non-metallic objects, keys, cans and other interesting items.

PD Provide multi-use outdoor equipment such as planks, boxes, steps, tunnels and so on, and encourage the children to explore and use the pieces of equipment whenever possible.

Self-confidence and self-esteem are vital to a child's all-round development. The activities within this chapter will boost these attributes by encouraging the children to talk about themselves and help them to understand and talk about their needs and feelings.

Don't be scared

What to do

■ Sit in a circle with the children and show them the teddy bear.

■ Explain that you are going to spend some time talking together and, to make sure that everyone has a turn, you will pass Ted around and whoever is holding him can speak while the others listen.

■ Ask the children to think about what it is like when you go to a new place for the first time and do not know anybody.

■ Pass Ted around and let each child speak.

■ Value each child's contributions and reiterate any significant remarks before moving Ted to the next child, for example, 'Yes, Samina, you're quite right, you might feel sad and lonely. Well done! Now I wonder what George thinks'.

■ When everyone has had a turn, ask the children to think about how they might help a newcomer to the setting to feel less isolated and alone.

■ Pass Ted around the circle again, listening to all the ideas and responding as before.

■ Draw the session to a close by summarising the various ideas and suggesting that the next time a new child arrives, you all put the children's ideas into practice.

■ Work in groups of two or three with younger children and be ready to help them with suggestions of your own.

■ Encourage older children to paint or draw posters to depict the welcoming ideas and display them to remind everyone how they can help.

More ideas

■ Invite potential new children to visit the group with their parents or carers several times before joining the group permanently.

■ Pair a new child with a more confident 'friend' to help them find their way around your setting and explain the routine to them.

Personal, social and emotional development

Goals for the Foundation Stage

Stepping Stone
Separate from main carer with support.

Early Learning Goal
Respond to significant experiences, showing a range of feelings when appropriate.

■

Group size
Whole group.

■

What you need
A teddy bear.

Home links
Encourage parents and carers to behave confidently themselves and not to show any of their own anxieties to their children. Tell them that you will call them later, if they are really worried, to confirm that their children have settled. (And then remember to do so!)

Other curriculum areas

CLL   Make name badges for the children to find and wear as soon as they arrive so that everyone knows each other's names.

MD   Number any doors such as the toilets or store cupboard, and label them with a picture to help new children find their way about.

Here I am

Early Learning Goal
Respond to significant experiences, showing a range of feelings when appropriate.

Group size
Individuals within whole group.

What you need
String; drawing pins; clothes pegs; a clearly-named cardboard teddy shape for each child.

Preparation
Fix a piece of string against a wall or across a window and add a peg for each child.
Assign a key worker to each child and make sure that both the child and their parent or carer know who their member of staff is.
Before each session begins, ensure that the key workers have the cardboard teddies for their assigned children and are ready to welcome them.

What to do
- As each child enters the setting, encourage them to hang up their coat, then go straight to their key worker to collect their teddy.
- Help the children to peg their teddy on the line to let everyone know that they are here before saying goodbye to their parent or carer, and then finding themselves an activity to do.

- Once all the children have arrived, gather them around and look together at the teddies on the piece of string.
- Invite each child to identify their own bear and confirm that they are here before counting all the bears and all the children.
- Make each bear different for use with younger children, to help with identification.
- Encourage older children to collect their bear from a central point and peg it up themselves.

More ideas
- Play name-remembering games such as 'Roll-a-ball'. Sit in a circle and roll a ball across to someone else and say, 'I'm Susan and I'm rolling the ball to Philip'.
- Encourage the children to help with cleaning up any mess, setting out equipment and packing away.

Home links
Make time to talk to every parent, carer and child either at the beginning or end of each session, even if it is only to say 'hello' or 'goodbye' on particularly busy days.

Other curriculum areas
KUW Make a simple pictorial timetable showing your basic daily routine. Copy the 'Our day' photocopiable sheet on page 85 and cut out the individual pictures. Glue them on to a 'Days of the week' chart to show the order of events each day. Add a feature of your own setting, such as music time or registration, to the blank space on the sheet. Encourage the children and parents and carers to refer to the chart each day.

PD Play 'Follow-the-leader', letting the children take turns to be the leader.

Who's this?

What to do

■ Display the photographs with suitable captions, for example, 'Mrs Soma is at her sister's wedding', 'Miss Leach is spending Christmas with her parents in Leicester'.

■ Gather the children around the collection of photographs and talk about them together.

■ Suggest that the display would be much more interesting if there were more photographs and ask the children if they think they might have a photograph of their family that they could bring to show to the group.

■ As each child brings in their photograph, talk about it with the child and together decide upon a suitable caption to display alongside it.

■ Every so often, gather the children together to look at the growing display and invite individual children to talk a little about their photograph and what is happening in it.

■ If possible, make enlarged colour photocopies of the photographs for use with younger children.

■ Encourage older children to write the names of the people shown in their photograph to display underneath.

More ideas

■ Use your circle times to talk about personal topics such as favourite foods, pets, favourite television programmes or books and so on.

■ Invite the children to take turns to rearrange the home corner so that it is more like their own home.

Other curriculum areas

KUW Give the children a disposable camera and invite them to take photographs of their friends playing in the group. Gradually build up a photograph album or collage showing the range of activities that you do in your setting.

CD Invite the children to draw or paint a picture of one particular room in their house and, as they work, encourage them to talk about what the room is used for and what is inside.

Stepping Stone
Talk freely about their home and community.

Early Learning Goal
Respond to significant experiences, showing a range of feelings when appropriate.

■

Group size
Whole group.

■

What you need
A family photograph or a photocopy from each member of staff; suitable display area.

Home links
Take the children for a walk around the local area, passing along the streets where they live, and encourage them to talk about the area and the people who live there.

Why are you afraid?

Stepping Stone
Express needs and feelings in appropriate ways.

■

Early Learning Goal
Respond to significant experiences, showing a range of feelings when appropriate.

■

Group size
Whole group.

■

What you need
A suitable story about being afraid such as *Can't You Sleep, Little Bear?* by Martin Waddell and Barbara Firth (Walker Books) or *Mr Jelly* by Roger Hargreaves (Egmont Books).

Home links
Before you carry out the activity, find out from parents and carers whether the children have any serious fears or phobias and, if so, how they deal with them at home.

What to do
■ Read the story to the children and talk about how Little Bear or Mr Jelly felt.

■ Have the children ever felt scared? What has scared them? What did they feel like when they were scared?

■ Talk about the fact that everyone is scared sometimes, but there are things that we can do to help ourselves feel better. What did Little Bear's Dad or Mr Jelly do? (Gave him more light./Counted to ten.)

■ Encourage the children to take turns to talk about their fears, and each time, ask the rest of the group to think of ways that they can chase away those fears.

■ Be aware that some younger children may become distressed just thinking about being scared, and may need a reassuring hug!

■ Encourage older children to concentrate on the effects of being scared rather than the cause of fear, for example, feeling shaky, cold, tearful and so on, and how you can feel better, for example, by having a hug, cuddling a favourite toy, singing a song and so on.

More ideas
■ Many story-books tackle subjects such as sadness, grief and bereavement, and these can be used as springboards for discussions about feelings. Remember to include the positive feelings of joy, happiness and excitement, too!

■ Make different facial expressions and let the children guess your mood and a possible reason for it.

Other curriculum areas

CD Listen to music depicting various moods and let the children try to make some sad or exciting sounds of their own using a selection of musical instruments.

CLL Invite the children to make books of 'Things that make me happy/sad/cross'. Encourage the children to draw or paint the pictures and to dictate some accompanying words for you to scribe underneath.

What's your name?

What to do

■ Show the children the teddy bear and remind them of when you talked about how to make new children feel welcome at your setting (see the activity 'Don't be scared' on page 29).

■ Spend a few moments recalling the things that you discussed, then invite a child to act as a welcomer.

■ Pretend to be a new child who is a little upset and frightened. Can the welcomer think of something to do to help, for example, introduce themselves to you and ask what your name is, invite you to play with a particular toy or game and so on.

■ Pair the children and encourage one to be the newcomer and one to be the welcomer.

■ Remind the children to stay in pairs until you say otherwise, and encourage them to talk to each other as they share the toys and activities and play together.

■ After a few minutes, gather all the children together again and talk about what you have been doing.

■ Praise the positive approaches and helpful attitudes that the children have displayed and repeat any particularly useful things that you saw the children doing, for example, 'When Jessica dripped her paint and was upset, it was very kind of Sammy to help her clean it up'.

■ Finish the session by repeating the activity and encourage the children to change roles.

■ Work with groups of only two or three younger children and let them each act as welcomer to a different teddy or soft toy.

■ Challenge older children to create short scenes that they can act out to the rest of the group.

More ideas

■ Set up a quiet area with cushions, books and cuddly toys where the children can go to unwind for a few minutes between more lively activities.

■ Use role-play to encourage playing fairly.

Stepping Stone
Separate from main carer with confidence.

Early Learning Goal
Have a developing awareness of their own needs, views and feelings and be sensitive to the needs, views and feelings of others.

■

Group size
Whole group.

■

What you need
A teddy bear.

Other curriculum areas

CLL — Invite the children to take an interest in others by asking them questions about themselves and what they like and dislike.

MD — Encourage the children to make pictures of themselves using gummed geometric shapes. Display them on a wall and connect friends with pieces of wool.

Home links
Find out from a new child's parents or carers whether there are any activities that they particularly like or dislike so that you can act accordingly.

Personal, social and emotional development

Be careful!

Stepping Stone
Show care and concern for self.

Early Learning Goal
Have a developing awareness of their own needs, views and feelings and be sensitive to the needs, views and feelings of others.

Group size
Whole group.

What you need
Simple equipment such as benches, mats, steps and boxes; large space.

Home links
Ask parents and carers to encourage their children to hang up their own coats when they arrive.

Other curriculum areas

KUW Make the home corner into a baby clinic and learn about health and personal hygiene.

PD Provide dressing-up clothes with a variety of fastenings such as buttons, zips, hooks, tie belts, buckles, Velcro, press-studs and so on.

What to do
- Set out the equipment in a safe and interesting way.
- Look at the equipment together and talk about how it might be used.
- Remind the children to look where they are going at all times and to try to notice where other people are so that they do not bump into each other and hurt someone.
- Set any rules that might be necessary, for example, only roll across a mat if it is empty, do not get too close to the person in front and so on. Talk to the children about why we need to have such rules.
- Invite the children to use the apparatus freely.
- Position yourself so that you have a good view of all the equipment and be ready with safety reminders.
- If a child asks for help to negotiate a piece of apparatus, try to help verbally at first, and only intervene physically if the child is in danger or is becoming distressed.
- At the end of the session, gather the children together and congratulate them on how well they did and remind them again of the rules that they were following.
- Try to have at least two adult helpers with younger children, so that one can observe while the other deals with any incidents.
- Show older children how to lift and carry the equipment safely so that they can begin to set it out for themselves.

More ideas
- Encourage the children to think about their own needs by asking questions such as 'We're going outside and it's very cold. What do we need to do?'.
- Show the children an enlarged copy of the 'Oh dear!' photocopiable sheet on page 86. Talk about how each picture shows everyday mishaps and how they could be prevented.

Personal, social and emotional development

Take care

What to do
■ Look at the picture of a distressed child together and discuss it.
■ Ask the children how they think the child is feeling. What might be causing their distress? How might their distress be relieved?
■ Lead the discussion towards how the children should ask for help if they need to. Encourage the children to think about what they should do in the following situations:
● they are out shopping and lose sight of their parent or carer
● they have broken one of their mum's best plates and the sharp pieces are all over the floor
● they are playing with their friend when they fall over and hurt themselves badly.
■ When you have discussed the various scenarios, invite the children to put on aprons and paint a picture of one of the situations, talking to them as they work.
■ Scribe a short description to accompany each painting.
■ Be ready to support younger children who may become distressed if the activity brings back painful memories.
■ Encourage older children to write their own descriptions to accompany their picture. Once the paintings are dry, attach their descriptions to them.

More ideas
■ Invite the local policeman or woman in to your setting to talk to the children about what they should do if they get lost.
■ Set up a hospital corner or a doctor's surgery and encourage the 'patients' to explain their ailments clearly to the 'doctor' so that they know how to treat them.

Stepping Stone
Express needs and feelings in appropriate ways.

Early Learning Goal
Have a developing awareness of their own needs, views and feelings and be sensitive to the needs, views and feelings of others.
■
Group size
Up to ten children.
■
What you need
A picture of a distressed child; paper; paint; paintbrushes; aprons.

Home links
Talk to parents and carers about their children's paintings and encourage them to continue the discussion at home.

Other curriculum areas
MD Learn this number rhyme and put actions to it.
One little girl was feeling sad,
Two little boys were feeling mad,
Three little girls were happy and bright,
Four little boys were scared of the night,
Five little children were tired as can be
So they went to sleep quickly
1... 2... 3...

KUW Have a selection of old telephones and show the children how to use them.

Tell us about it

Stepping Stone
Talk freely about their home and community.

Early Learning Goal
Have a developing respect for their own cultures and beliefs and those of other people.

Group size
Whole group.

What you need
A collection of large, clear photographs of relevant places of worship, indoors and outdoors if possible; artefacts of religious events or ceremonies relating to them.

Preparation
Ensure that you have a good knowledge of the group's ethnic and religious background as well as the relevant major festivals and ceremonies.

What to do
■ Gather the children together and show them a photograph of a place of worship or an artefact relating to a religious event or ceremony.
■ Ask the children if anyone recognises it. Would anyone like to say anything about it?
■ If a child would like to talk about the photograph or artefact, pass it to them and encourage them to tell the group as much as they can about it.
■ Thank the child for their valuable contribution before moving on to the next item.
■ Work your way through all the photographs and artefacts, encouraging as many children as possible to join in.
■ Finally, give the relevant item to each child who spoke and invite them to stand at the front of the group while you give a brief résumé of each photograph or artefact and talk about the faith to which it refers.
■ Younger children may need considerable prompting, so make sure that you gather plenty of background information from parents or carers before you begin.
■ Encourage older children to ask the child that is speaking questions, and help them to find any answers that the child might have been unable to provide.

More ideas
■ Ensure that your home corner reflects the ethnic balance of your group by providing appropriate dressing-up clothes, furniture and props.
■ Provide a good supply of picture books about houses and homes and use them to initiate discussions about the children's own homes.

Other curriculum areas
KUW Make a collection of recipes from around the world and invite the children to make some of them.

CLL Create a group newspaper. Invite the children to draw pictures of what they have been doing, then use a computer and printer to type the children's news to go alongside their drawings.

Home links
Choose a theme, such as 'Babies', and invite parents and carers from various backgrounds to provide photographs or artefacts, or to come in to talk to the children about related events such as baptism and choosing a name.

Personal, social and emotional development

Let's dance

What to do
■ Gather the children together and choose a set of music tapes, costumes and instruments to explore.
■ Pass the instruments around and encourage each child to make a sound with them.
■ Listen to some of the tape together and invite the children to identify any of the instruments that are being used.
■ Put the instruments and tape to one side while you introduce the costumes and talk about who might wear them and how they are worn.

■ Once everyone is familiar with all the props, turn on the tape again and invite the group to dress up, to dance to the music and to play the instruments freely.
■ Remain close at hand to talk to the children about what they are doing and to share the books with them when they stop for a rest.
■ Join in with younger children to encourage them to feel and enjoy the rhythm of the music.
■ Encourage older children to invent a sequence of movements, then make up a little dance to do with their friends.

More ideas
■ Invite relevant members of the local community in to demonstrate how to wear a sari, play an instrument or make unleavened bread.
■ Build up a collection of video clips showing different lifestyles from around the world and regularly watch and discuss them together.

Other curriculum areas
KUW Store the tape recorder or CD player alongside tapes or CDs of stories, as well as music, from around the world. Teach the children how to use it themselves so that they are able to make their own choices.
CD Let the children use the real musical instruments as inspiration for making their own instruments using recyclable materials.

Stepping Stone
Have a sense of self as a member of different communities.

Early Learning Goal
Have a developing respect for their own cultures and beliefs and those of other people.
■
Group size
Up to six children.
■
What you need
Tape recorder or CD player; sets of music tapes or CDs; costumes and instruments, each with a different cultural background; an open space indoors or outdoors, where the children can move freely to music; relevant, colourful story-books and picture books.

Home links
Ask parents and carers if they can play an instrument, such as a violin, sitar, Spanish guitar or steel drum and if they would be willing to give a demonstration to the group.

Personal, social and emotional development

You are invited

Stepping Stone
Initiate interactions with other people.

Early Learning Goal
Have a developing respect for their own cultures and beliefs and those of other people.
■

Group size
Whole group at first, then small groups of 'hosts' and 'guests'.
■

What you need
Multicultural home-corner equipment.

Home links
Invite the children's grandparents in to your story corner and ask them to talk to the children about how life was when they were children.

What to do
■ Explain to the children that they are going to take turns to invite friends to the home corner.
■ Talk about why visitors come to our houses, for example, to share a meal, join a celebration, stay overnight, enjoy a cup of tea and a chat.
■ Discuss how we should behave when we are guests, and how to make guests feel welcome when we are hosts.
■ Invite two children to be hosts. Encourage the rest of the children to carry out other activities while preparations are being made. Tell them that you will come to collect the guests when everything is ready.
■ Talk to the hosts about who will be coming to their house and why. Discuss the necessary preparations and help them to arrange the furniture and equipment in the home corner accordingly.
■ When everything is almost ready, talk to the children about how to welcome their guests and make them feel comfortable.
■ Act as 'chauffeur' and go to collect the guests while the hosts stay at home awaiting their arrival and making last minute preparations.
■ As you accompany the guests to the house, talk again about how they should behave in other people's homes, reminding them how to be polite and well-mannered.
■ Suggest that younger children might invite a teddy rather than a child to tea at first, until they feel more confident.
■ Encourage older children to design invitations to send to their guests.

More ideas
■ Provide dual-language books to help the children understand that there are many different languages in the world.
■ Make a telephone from a length of hosepipe and two funnels. Place a bell nearby so that the children can pick up one end and ring the bell for someone else to pick up the other end.

Other curriculum areas
PD Provide see-saws, passenger-carrying vehicles and other equipment that work best when used by more than one child.

MD Find out about patterns from various cultural backgrounds and try to copy some of them.

For many children, joining your setting may be their first opportunity to form relationships outside their family. This chapter aims to help to develop this ability by introducing games to play with the children and encourage them to take part in larger group activities.

Please take care of it

What to do

- Gather the children together and show them your personal belonging.
- Explain that although it is not worth a lot of money, it is very precious to you. Briefly say what makes it so special.
- Tell the children that you would like them to handle your personal belonging themselves, but that you do not want it spoiled so you would like them to be very careful with it.
- Pass the item around the children, inviting them to ask questions about it and reminding them to handle it with care.
- When the object makes its way back to you, display it in a safe but accessible place for the children to see, and add your name and a short explanatory note. Tell the children that they may look at it, but not touch it, for the rest of the session.
- Suggest to the children that they bring in a favourite book or toy from home to share with the group and say that you will all take special care of it.
- Each time that a child brings an object from home, repeat the activity and display the precious item on the 'safe shelf', sending it home with the child at the end of the session.
- If a younger child is reluctant to leave his toy on display, use an upturned aquarium as a display case.
- Encourage older children to make their own labels and notes for their personal belongings.

More ideas

- Encourage reluctant children to chat by playing alongside them and talking aloud to yourself about what you are doing.
- Provide old telephones for the children to use in the home corner.

Other curriculum areas

CD   Play singing games, such as 'Row, Row, Row Your Boat' or 'See Saw Margery Daw', in which the children will need to trust their partners not to let go as they rock back and forth.

CLL   Make puppets regularly available to encourage verbal interaction between the children.

Goals for the **Foundation Stage**

Stepping Stone
Feel safe and secure and demonstrate a sense of trust.

Early Learning Goal
Form good relationships with adults and peers.

Group size
Whole group.

What you need
A personal belonging to share with the group; the children's personal belongings.

Home links
Make time to see every parent and carer for a few minutes at least once a week to talk about their child.

Find your other half

Early Learning Goal
Form good relationships with adults and peers.

Group size
Up to 12 children.

What you need
Large space to move around in; the 'Farmyard friends' photocopiable sheet on page 87.

Preparation
Be aware that some animals may be unacceptable in certain cultures so check this before you carry out this activity. Copy the photocopiable sheet on to card, colour it in and cut out the pictures.

What to do
■ Gather the group together and look at the animal pictures in turn, ensuring that the children know what each animal is.
■ Explain that you are going to play a partner-finding game with the cards, but that first you need to cut them in half.
■ Cut some pictures in half vertically, and some horizontally, before shuffling them all together.

■ Invite the children to spread out around the room and give each child half of a picture.
■ Tell the children to look carefully at their half of the animal and decide what it is.
■ Invite them to walk around the room looking at other halves of pictures until they find their matching animal.
■ When they have a complete picture, encourage them to sit on the floor with their partner.
■ Encourage younger children to move around the room by gently taking their hand and walking with them.
■ Challenge older children to hide their pictures and make the relevant animal sound to find their partner.
■ Finish the session by checking all the pictures and congratulate the children on finding the matching ones.
■ Sing together 'Old MacDonald Had a Farm' from *This Little Puffin...* compiled by Elizabeth Matterson (Puffin Books).

Home links
Encourage the children to share their experiences with each other by bringing in models or pictures that they have made at home, photographs of special family events, or swimming or dancing badges and certificates that they may have earned.

Other curriculum areas
PD Encourage the children to work together by providing huge cardboard boxes for construction.

MD Act out 'Five Currant Buns in a Baker's Shop' from *This Little Puffin...* compiled by Elizabeth Matterson (Puffin Books).

More ideas
■ Regularly gather the children together at the end of a session and encourage them to tell each other what they have been doing and show any pictures or models that they have made.
■ Display the children's work prominently and encourage them to tell their parents, carers and friends how they did it or demonstrate how it works.

Sarah wants a friend

Stepping Stone
Relate and make attachments to members of their group.

Early Learning Goal
Form good relationships with adults and peers.

Group size
Whole group.

What you need
A large space for the children to move around in a circle.

What to do
■ Stand together in a circle, holding hands.
■ Explain to the children that you are going to play a game and invite a child to go into the middle of the ring to start it off.
■ Ask the rest of the children who is in the middle of the ring. When they all call that child's name, tell them that this is what the game is called, for example, 'Sarah's in the ring'.
■ As you walk round to the left, sing 'Sarah's in the ring, Sarah's in the ring, E-I-E-I, Sarah's in the ring' to the tune of 'The Farmer's in his Dell'. Then stop, jump to face the centre and jump again to face to the right.
■ Walk round to the right singing, 'Sarah wants a friend, Sarah wants a friend, E-I-E-I, Sarah wants a friend'.
■ Stop, jump to face the centre and let Sarah choose a friend. She should then rejoin the circle and the game continues with a new child in the centre.
■ With younger children let the first child stay in the centre, and continue the game until there are five children in the middle.
■ Encourage older children to describe the friend that they are choosing instead of just naming them.

More ideas
■ Suggest that the children help each other to do up coats and shoes.
■ Take the children for a walk in the local area and invite the children to walk in pairs so that they can talk to each other as they go.

Home links
Display a list of all the children who attend the group so that parents and carers can refer to it when talking to their child or addressing party invitations and Christmas cards.

Other curriculum areas
MD Help the children to discover things they have in common by making a 'Birthday board' to show when the children were born.
KUW Let the children make a pizza and invite friends to share it with them.

It's party time

What to do

■ Tell the children that you are going to have a party and you would like them to help with the preparations.

■ Help each child to create a hat made from cardboard and decorate it with shiny, sparkly or dangly materials. Display or store them until the party.

■ Invite the children to make wrist or ankle bands using strips of card decorated with shredded tissue paper and glitter.

■ Let the children make shakers using yoghurt pots and rice or pasta. Decorate them vibrantly and put them aside until your Mardi Gras party.

■ On the day of the party, start the session normally to let the children settle and dedicate just the final half an hour or so to the party.

■ Gather the children together and read *Nini at Carnival* before explaining a little about Mardi Gras and telling them that it is now time for their party.

■ Give out the hats and wristbands to the children while the music plays very quietly.

■ Turn the music up slightly, give the children their shakers and invite them to dance around the room.

■ Have a quiet corner available where younger children can observe until they feel ready to join in.

■ Encourage older children to do a simple circle dance by going into the middle and out again, round to the left, round to the right, round to the left and start again.

■ After a while, turn the music very low and gather the children together to enjoy the crisps, biscuits and squash.

■ Bring the party to a close by giving 'Three cheers for Mardi Gras' and having a mini siesta until parents and carers arrive!

More ideas

■ Plan regular celebrations throughout the year to cover a variety of events.

■ Arrange an afternoon when the children can serve biscuits and squash to their grandparents, parents and carers and invite them to stay and play.

Other curriculum areas

KUW Make regular visits to local places such as the library, park, places of worship and so on. Talk about how to behave when you get there.

PD Enlist extra adult support to take a group of children to the local swimming baths.

Home links
Invite parents and carers to help the children to make the hats, wristbands and shakers.

Personal, social and emotional development

Stay close

What to do

■ Gather the children together and talk about any shopping trips that the children may have been on to busy shopping centres and markets. Discuss how easy it is to get lost or separated from their family.

■ Talk about what they should do if they get lost, for example, where they might go for help. (Police officer, security guard or shop assistant.)

■ Explain that the police officer, security guard or the shop assistant will call their parents over the tannoy.

■ Invite some of the children to play the parts of shop assistants, police officers, or security guards and shoppers, while you take on the part of the lost child.

■ Act out a short scene to the rest of the group where the child becomes separated from the family, seeks help, then is reunited with their parents.

■ Talk briefly about the scene, reinforcing the main points and reminding the children that they should not keep wandering in search of their parents, but should go to a uniformed person or a shop assistant for help.

■ Invite groups of children to use the role-play area in turn, each time taking a different role as you play alongside them.

■ Support younger children by taking the part of an older sibling and guiding them through the correct procedures.

■ Encourage older children to devise a simple set of rules about avoiding getting lost or getting help if they do get lost.

Other curriculum areas

CLL Encourage the children to practise saying their first and last names loudly and clearly.

MD Invite the children to count slowly to ten or more in situations requiring patience or self-control.

More ideas

■ Set up an area with a zebra crossing and practise using it safely.

■ Hold regular fire drills so that the children know exactly what to do in the case of a real fire.

Stepping Stone
Value and contribute to own well-being and self-control.

Early Learning Goal
Form good relationships with adults and peers.
■
Group size
Whole group during the introduction, then up to eight children for the role-play.
■
What you need
Role-play area set up as shopping centre; police officers' helmets; security guards' hats; appropriate dressing-up clothes and props.

Home links
Give each child a copy of the 'Lost and found!' photocopiable sheet on page 88 to take home. Ask parents and carers to play the game with their children and talk to them about getting lost while shopping. Encourage them to make sure that their children understand what to do and can recite their names clearly. If they have a mobile phone, suggest that their children could keep the number in their pocket.

Parachute game

Stepping Stone
Feel safe and secure and demonstrate a sense of trust.

Early Learning Goal
Work as part of a group or class, taking turns and sharing fairly, understanding that there needs to be agreed values and codes of behaviour for groups of people, including adults and children, to work together harmoniously.

Group size
Whole group.

What you need
A play parachute or a large piece of lightweight material; large open space; at least three adult helpers.

Home links
Explain to parents and carers that you have been encouraging the children to work together and ask them to play games with their children that involve turn-taking.

What to do

■ Spread out the parachute and invite the children to sit around its perimeter without touching the parachute.

■ Ensure that the adults are evenly spread among the children.

■ Explain to the children that you are going to play some parachute games, so they all need to listen very carefully so that everyone works together.

■ Ask the children to adopt a kneeling position and grasp the parachute edge firmly in an overhand grip, keeping it close to the ground.

■ Tell them that the parachute is like a pond and the water is very still and calm. Can they see how still it is?

■ Then say that a little breeze is blowing across the surface, and gently shake the parachute to make ripples.

■ Gradually build up the movement until there is a raging storm and the parachute is heaving furiously.

■ Then let the storm gradually subside until the parachute is flat on the floor once more.

■ Repeat the activity several times, constantly encouraging the children to listen carefully to instructions and to work together all the time.

■ Ensure that younger children are next to an adult to support them verbally throughout.

■ Invite an older child to take over as group leader and conduct a storm from beginning to end.

More ideas

■ Build up the children's trust by playing parachute games involving most of the group supporting the parachute while a selected few children run under the parachute to emerge at the opposite side.

■ Use sand-timers to ensure that the children take it in turns fairly, for example, one, three or five minutes as appropriate.

Other curriculum areas

PD Put sponge balls on to a parachute with a hole in the centre and work together to shake, bounce and roll them through the hole.

CD Encourage the children to work together by providing long sheets of paper for them to create group murals or collages.

Personal, social and emotional development

Would you like some?

What to do

■ Ensure that the children thoroughly wash their hands and that work surfaces and equipment are perfectly clean.

■ Tell the children that they are going to make some sandwiches to share with a friend and ask them to think about who they would like that friend to be.

■ Look at the ingredients and help the children to decide which fillings their friends might like.

■ Give each child a blunt knife and invite them to make a round of sandwiches, cut them into quarters and arrange them on a plate.

■ Then help the children to set the table for their friends and make up some fruit squash.

■ When all the preparations are complete, let the children invite their friends to share their food.

■ When the tea party is over and the guests have departed, help the remaining hosts to work together to wash up, pack away the equipment and tidy the area.

■ Accompany younger children to support them when they go to invite their friend.

■ Encourage older children to work out a job roster so that they can work together efficiently to clear away.

More ideas

■ Give the children regular opportunities to choose a friend to share an activity by telling them that there is space for one child and a friend.

■ Encourage the children to bring in news from home to share with the rest of the group.

Other curriculum areas

CD When a child has completed a picture or model, encourage them to show it to a friend and see if they want to make one, too.

CLL Gather the group together mid-session and encourage each child to tell the rest of the group what they have been doing and what they have enjoyed about the activity.

Stepping Stone
Seek out others to share experiences.

Early Learning Goal
Work as part of a group or class, taking turns and sharing fairly, understanding that there needs to be agreed values and codes of behaviour for groups of people, including adults and children, to work together harmoniously.

Group size
Two or four children.

What you need
Hygienic space for food preparation; bread; margarine or butter; jam; cheese spread; blunt knife; plates; cups; fruit squash; jug; table; chairs; table-cloth; washing-up facilities.

Preparation
Check for any food allergies and dietary requirements.

Home links
Hold a family picnic day and encourage everyone to bring along food and drink to share with each other.

Ding-ding – we're off!

Early Learning Goal
Work as part of a group or class, taking turns and sharing fairly, understanding that there needs to be agreed values and codes of behaviour for groups of people, including adults and children, to work together harmoniously.

Group size
Up to ten children.

What you need
Chairs; cardboard disc or steering wheel; driver's hat or badge; bus stop sign; tickets; felt-tipped pens; pieces of A4 card; dressing-up clothes.

Home links
Ask the children to bring in any photographs of journeys that they have made on buses, boats, planes or trains. Encourage them to talk about their journeys to their friends.

What to do

■ Tell the children that you are going to create a bus. Talk about who might go on the bus and where it might take them.

■ Write a different destination on each piece of card, adding a small pictorial clue to aid recognition.

■ Encourage three or four children to arrange the chairs to make a bus and another child to position the bus stop.

■ Invite a child to take the first turn as the driver, display the destination card and invite the passengers to get on the bus or wait at the bus stop.

■ As play unfolds, encourage the children to talk to fellow passengers or join together to form family groups.

■ Talk to them about who they are, where they are going and what they are going to do when they get there.

■ Support younger children by accompanying them on the bus and suggesting alternative places to visit or things to do.

■ Encourage older children to make their own destination cards to display.

More ideas

■ Make a 'friendship ring' by choosing one child to start it off. Encourage them to choose a friend to hold their hand and so on, until a circle is formed. The first child then starts a chant that continues around the circle, for example, 'I'm Annie and my friend is Jake, I'm Jake and my friend is Ahmed' and so on.

■ Encourage the children to draw pictures for each other and attempt to write their friend's name.

Other curriculum areas

KUW Take the children for a short trip on a real bus and encourage them to watch people queuing and taking turns to get on and off the bus.

MD Help the children to find out more about each other by conducting surveys about favourite foods, activities or stories and displaying the results in a pictogram.

Listen carefully

What to do

■ Select an instrument and stand facing the children.

■ Explain to the children that you would like them to skip, dance and jig around the room, but they must listen very carefully all the time, because when you bang the drum/strike the triangle, they must stand still and raise their hands high in the air.

■ Play the game a few times to ensure that all the children know what to do.

■ Then invite a child to take your place at the front of the group.

■ Ask them to choose an instrument and decide what they want everyone to do when they play it, for example, stand on one leg, sit down, make a funny face and so on.

■ Play the game several times then encourage the child playing the instrument to select a different leader for the next round.

■ Continue playing the game for as long as the children remain interested, or until most of the children, who want to, have had a turn to lead the game.

■ Work alongside younger children to offer verbal support as necessary.

■ Invite older children to select two or more instruments and invent a different action for each one.

More ideas

■ Regularly provide changes to your routine by inviting visitors to your setting to read stories, demonstrate a craft, play an instrument or perform a dance.

■ Take the children to visit a local retirement home to sing songs for the residents.

Other curriculum areas

CD If possible, enlist the help of adult support and take the children to a suitable production at a local theatre.

PD Hold a sponsored walk to raise funds for your group and to highlight the importance of exercise to keep us healthy.

Stepping Stone
Demonstrate flexibility and adapt their behaviour to different events, social situations and changes in routine.

Early Learning Goal
Work as part of a group or class, taking turns and sharing fairly, understanding that there needs to be agreed values and codes of behaviour for groups of people, including adults and children, to work together harmoniously.

Group size
Up to ten children.

What you need
A small selection of percussion instruments; large space to move freely.

Home links
Hold a mini concert and invite parents and carers in to watch.

Personal, social and emotional development

Who's next?

Early Learning Goal
Work as part of a group or class, taking turns and sharing fairly, understanding that there needs to be agreed values and codes of behaviour for groups of people, including adults and children, to work together harmoniously.

Group size
Four to six children.

What you need
Large wooden beads; laces; large dice (adapted to show only 1, 2 and 3).

What to do
■ Explain to the children that you are going to play a game that involves collecting beads and everyone will be taking turns to roll a dice to see how many they can collect.
■ Give each child a lace and explain that the object of the game is to collect ten beads on the lace in total.
■ Select a child to start the game and ask them to roll the dice and tell you how many beads they need according to the number on the dice.
■ If they count the dots accurately and ask for the correct amount, give them the beads. If they count incorrectly, ask the rest of the group to help them try again before giving them the beads.
■ While the child is threading the beads, the next player should roll the dice.
■ Occasionally pause the game to check how many beads each child has and how many more they need.
■ Play continues until all the children have ten beads each.
■ Let younger children collect a lace full of beads rather than a designated number.
■ With older children, add a zero to the dice to help them learn to cope with the frustration of effectively missing a turn.

More ideas
■ Let the children play simple relay races involving waiting to receive an object before they can run.
■ Ask the children to report anything that they consider might be dangerous in their environment, such as protruding nails in fences, stinging nettles close to the path and so on, so that they can be investigated and dealt with.

Other curriculum areas
CLL Encourage self-control by asking the children to carry out a particular instruction, for example, invite all the children on the red table to go to wash their hands. Give the children specific information to tell their parents such as 'I need to bring my wellingtons tomorrow'.
KUW Provide opportunities for the children to use simple wood-working equipment in a safe and controlled manner.

One of the hardest lessons that any child will probably have to learn is that they cannot have their own way all of the time. This chapter provides activities to encourage the children to learn to accept and follow rules as necessary.

When is it my turn?

What to do

■ Gather the children around the toys and ask who would like to ride them. Hopefully they will all want to!

■ Ask the children if they think that there are enough vehicles for everyone to have one each.

■ Invite the children to tell you what can be done to solve the problem, for example, get another toy out or take turns to play with the toys.

■ Explain that it is not possible to get another toy out today, so taking turns seems like a good idea. Ask the children for suggestions as to how this might be done fairly.

■ Show the children the sand-timer and how it works.

■ Give the vehicles to three children and the timer to the child without a vehicle, asking them to tell you when the sand has run through.

■ At the end of that time, invite the child without a vehicle to choose one and to give the timer to its rider.

■ Continue in this manner, enlisting the children's help to make sure that there is a good rotation of toys and children.

■ With younger children, use three very similar toys to avoid conflict.

■ Encourage older children to work out a fair rotation system for themselves instead of using a timer.

More ideas

■ Help the children to create a set of rules for using wheeled toys.

■ If a child breaks the rules, ask them if they know what they have done wrong and what they think they can do to put it right.

Other curriculum areas

 CD   During art and craft activities, regularly put out less resources than there are children.

PD   Practise throwing-and-catching activities in pairs to promote collaborative play.

Personal, social and emotional development

Picnic time

Early Learning Goal
Understand what is right, what is wrong, and why.

Group size
Small groups initially; whole group for picnic.

What you need
Plastic knives; bread; butter or margarine; sandwich fillings; paper plates; biscuits; fruit; plastic cups; squash; foil; paper bags; cardboard boxes; blankets; safe outdoor area; the 'Litter pick' photocopiable sheet on page 89.

Preparation
Check for any food allergies or dietary requirements.

Home links
Ask parents and carers to encourage their children to design an anti-litter poster at home and bring it in to show to the group.

What to do

- Work with small groups of children to prepare and pack the picnic, involving as many of the children in the activity a s possible.
- When everything is ready, ask the children to carry the food and blankets carefully to the desired spot.
- Invite the children to spread out the blankets and sit down.
- Encourage the children to unwrap the plates of food and pass them around, and to share out the drinks and fruit.

- When everyone has finished eating, stand up and look at the area. Talk to the children about what you can see.
- If some of the children have tidied their litter or put it into one of the boxes, praise them enthusiastically and encourage the other children to do the same.
- When everything is tidy, sit down with the children and talk about what to do with the rubbish, and why.
- Talk about the fact that although food rots, it does not look very pleasant left lying on the ground. Ask the children to think of a better place to put the rubbish.
- Be ready to point out litter to younger children as they sometimes overlook things that are right in front of them.
- When you return to the setting, give older children a copy of the photocopiable sheet and ask them to put a circle around each piece of litter that they can see.

Other curriculum areas

CD Learn the rhyme 'Don't drop litter – put it in the bin!' from *Bobby Shaftoe, Clap Your Hands* by Sue Nicholls (A & C Black) and make up some verses of your own.

KUW Use magnets to test grocery tins and drinks cans to see which are recyclable.

More ideas

- Consider having a pet that the children can care for at home during weekends and holidays.
- Have a spring-cleaning session when the children can help to clean tables, wash plastic toys and generally take care of their immediate environment.

Personal, social and emotional development

Dig it up

What to do

■ Tell the children that you are going to do some gardening and discuss why this is necessary.

■ Talk about weeds and how they take the goodness from the soil that other plants need to grow.

■ Explain to the children why they should never uproot plants without an adult's permission.

■ Take the children to look at the area that needs weeding. Ask them if anyone can see anything they think should not be growing there? (Dandelions, grasses, thistles, nettles.)

■ Talk about the need to wear gloves because some plants sting, have thorns or are poisonous.

■ Identify a particular type of weed and invite the children to take turns to find and remove one just the same, putting the uprooted plant into the wheelbarrow.

■ Continue in this way until the area is free of weeds, encouraging the children to talk to you about what they are doing as they work.

■ Invite a child to tip the contents of the wheelbarrow in a suitable place and congratulate the children on a job well done.

■ Remind them all to wash their hands even though they have been wearing gloves.

■ Loosen the soil slightly around the weeds for younger children before they try to pull them up.

■ Show older children how to loosen the soil around the weeds and encourage them to do this by themselves.

More ideas

■ Take regular walks around your location and talk about things that are spoiling it such as graffiti, litter, overgrown land, broken fences and so on.

■ Set up a rota and invite the children to take turns to collect litter using special grabbers and wearing gloves. (Always remind the children not to touch any broken glass or sharp objects that they may find, and to always ask an adult to remove them instead.)

Stepping Stone
Show care and concern for others, for living things and the environment.

Early Learning Goal
Understand what is right, what is wrong, and why.

■

Group size
Up to four children.

■

What you need
Protective gloves; toy wheelbarrow or truck; small hand tools or old kitchen spoons and forks; small outdoor area or tub that requires weeding.

Home links
Encourage parents and carers to let their children hang up their own coats when they arrive, and to take responsibility for any other property that they may bring to the setting.

Other curriculum areas

MD Invite the children to plant and look after sunflower seeds, measuring them every week as they grow.

KUW Set up a bird table and encourage the children to feed and provide water for the birds in winter, and make a bath for them in summer.

Personal, social and emotional development

Tunnel around

Stepping Stone
Show confidence and the ability to stand up for own rights.

Early Learning Goal
Understand what is right, what is wrong, and why.

Group size
Four children.

What you need
A large, deep tray of damp sand; small rustproof vehicles.

What to do

■ Suggest to the children that it might be fun to work together to make some tunnels in the sand.

■ Explain to the children that you would like them to dig the tunnels with their hands.

■ As they make the tunnels, suggest that they might work together, perhaps from opposite ends to make a longer tunnel, or maybe by joining all the tunnels together to form a network.

■ If any disagreements arise, give the children time to settle them amicably themselves. However, if you need to intervene, or one child begins to dominate the whole group, stop the children from digging and ask everyone to reflect upon their behaviour and consider whether there might be a better way to sort things out.

■ Encourage the children to think of a solution for themselves and to negotiate verbally rather than reacting physically.

■ When the tray is full of tunnels, give the children the vehicles and let them use them freely in the sand before ending the session.

■ Support younger children by suggesting suitable phrases to use or action to take if they feel that they are being treated unfairly.

■ Set a specific challenge for older children that will require them to collaborate, for example, 'Build six tunnels that join together in the middle' or 'Build two tunnels that cross in the middle'.

More ideas

■ Develop the children's self-esteem by creating a photograph album of their achievements such as cooking, climbing, building, painting and so on. Label each photograph with a positive caption.

■ Play 'Pass a compliment' at circle time by taking turns to make a positive remark about the person to your left.

Home links
Regularly share the children's social as well as practical achievements with parents and carers at the end of a session.

Other curriculum areas

CLL Act out favourite stories to practise being bold, timid, brave, fierce or dominating and talk about what each one feels like.

CD Let the children practise taking a leading role by challenging them to work in pairs, each taking a turn to make a picture or pattern for the other one to copy.

Personal, social and emotional development

Out and about

What to do

◼ Explain to the children that you are all going to go for a walk and spend some time talking about appropriate behaviour.

◼ Carry out the usual preparations, such as going to the toilets, putting on coats, doing up shoelaces and so on, before inviting the children to choose a partner to walk with.

◼ Encourage the children to talk to each other about where they are and what they can see as they walk.

◼ As you walk, constantly praise the way that the children are keeping together and walking to one side of the pavement, not too close to the kerb or the road.

◼ If anyone starts walking too fast, or behaving inappropriately in any way, stop the whole group and talk about why you have had to stop, encouraging the children to think about things for themselves, rather than just instructing them.

◼ If a child continues to behave badly, insist that they hold your hand and let their partner make up a group of three.

◼ With very young children, take only two at first, gradually increasing the number as they show they can be trusted.

◼ With older children, practise crossing a quiet road by acting as a crossing warden, going into the road first, then signalling the children across, emphasising that they should wait for you on the other side.

More ideas

◼ Regularly target different areas of behaviour to remind the children to say please and thank you, to talk in a quiet voice, to say excuse me please and so on. Remember to constantly model such language yourself!

◼ Keep a supply of reward stickers and give them out every now and then for excellent behaviour, explaining why you have done so, for example, 'Well done, Harmeet, you said "Excuse me" when you wanted to get past!'.

Other curriculum areas

CLL Begin a story about someone who does something wrong, such as runs away from their parents while shopping or never lets anyone share their toys, and invite the children to finish it.

PD Play games with the children that require simple rules. Discuss the rules and the reasons why they should be obeyed, both before and after each game.

Stepping Stone
Have an awareness of the boundaries set and behavioural expectations within the setting.

Early Learning Goal
Understand what is right, what is wrong, and why.
◼
Group size
Up to eight children.
◼
What you need
An adult helper; mobile phone, if possible.

Home links
Enlarge and display the 'Learning partnership' photocopiable sheet on page 90 to inform parents and carers regarding the expectations and boundaries in your setting.

Personal, social and emotional development

Horrid or kind?

Early Learning Goal
Consider the consequences of their words and actions for themselves and others.

■

Group size
Whole group.

■

What you need
A teddy bear or similar.

Home links
Encourage the children to greet their parents and carers pleasantly when they arrive to collect them, and practise phrases that they might use.

What to do

■ Gather the children into a circle and tell them that you are going to play a game called 'Horrid or kind', and that you are going to take turns to say something to Teddy.

■ Start the game off by holding Teddy in front of you and talking directly to him, for example, 'Your fur is all smelly!'.

■ Ask the children what they thought about how you spoke to Teddy and how they think Teddy feels. How do the children think you should make amends?

■ Explain to the children that Teddy needs to hear something kind now and pass him to a child to say something to cheer him up.

■ Again discuss what was said and think about the effect that it might have had on Teddy.

■ Continue to pass Teddy around the circle, taking turns to say something to him. Each time talk about what was said.

■ To keep a positive atmosphere each time that Teddy is spoken to unkindly, make sure that the child apologises, and that the next statement is kind.

■ Be aware that younger children may become upset on Teddy's behalf so be ready to reassure them that it is only a game.

■ Talk about 'white lies' with older children, explaining that sometimes telling the truth can be hurtful.

More ideas

■ Set up a hospital role-play area and encourage the 'doctors' and 'nurses' to treat their 'patients' with care and concern.

■ Involve the children in raising money to help local charities, for example, organise a sponsored walk or a sponsored quiz.

Other curriculum areas

KUW As part of a 'Senses' project, learn about major disabilities, such as deafness or blindness, and find out how to help those suffering from them.

MD Draw a number line showing things to make other people happy, for example, one big hug, two little kisses, three pretty pictures, four favourite sweets, five beautiful flowers and so on.

Who lives here?

What to do

■ Gather the children together and spend some time looking at the books and talking about the different creatures in them.

■ Suggest to the children that you keep a minibeast indoors for a few days and stress that it must be looked after carefully.

■ Give each child a small collecting jar and go outside to explore your natural environment.

■ Encourage the children to look under stones, logs or hedges to see what they can find.

■ Decide which creature to keep in your setting, for example, a slug, snail, worm, caterpillar or spider, and talk about how to take care of it.

■ When you are sure that the children understand how to look after the chosen minibeast, ask a child to carefully collect it into their jar.

■ Invite other children to collect soil in their jars for the bottom of the tank and vegetable matter from immediate surroundings.

■ Back indoors, set up the tank, put the creature inside it and secure the ventilated lid.

■ Ask the children to wash their hands thoroughly.

■ Check the tank every day to make sure that the minibeast is healthy and the environment is damp but not soggy. (At the first signs of distress or unhealthiness, release the minibeast.)

■ After three or four days, gather the children together and release the creature back to where you found it, talking to them about the reasons for doing this.

■ Give younger children an old spoon to carefully scoop up the soil and the creature together.

■ Encourage older children to observe the creature closely and to make a detailed drawing of it.

More ideas

■ Invite a local vet in to talk to the children about how to care for animals.

■ Grow some beansprouts or cress for the children to eat it. (Check for any food allergies and dietary requirements.)

Stepping Stone
Show care and concern for others, for living things and the environment.

Early Learning Goal
Consider the consequences of their words and actions for themselves and others.

■

Group size
Up to six children.

■

What you need
Natural outdoor environment; small collecting jars; small transparent plastic tank with a ventilated lid; books about minibeasts; old spoon; drawing equipment.

Home links
Invite the children to take turns to bring any suitable pet from home for a day, such as a gerbil, guinea pig, rabbit or budgie, and encourage them to tell their friends how to look after it.

Other curriculum areas

| CLL | Make zigzag books about how to care for different creatures. |
| PD | Practise moving like a variety of animals. |

Personal, social and emotional development

Look at me

Stepping Stone
Show confidence and the ability to stand up for own rights.

Early Learning Goal
Consider the consequences of their words and actions for themselves and others.

Group size
Up to six children.

What you need
The 'This is me' photocopiable sheet on page 91; scissors; colouring materials; collage materials; glue.

What to do

■ Copy the photocopiable sheet on to thin card for each child and explain that you would like them to make it look like themselves.

■ Talk about what they will need to add, for example, facial features, hair and clothes, and encourage them to look at the materials available.

■ Explain to the children that there are not enough glue sticks or scissors for everyone, so it will be necessary to share.

■ Remind the children that sharing is not making someone else wait until you have completely finished with something, but that it is about continually taking turns.

■ Tell the children that they must ask politely when they need to use something or nobody will know that they want it.

■ Talk about being patient as well as polite and ask the children what phrases they should use to get a particular item.

■ As the children work, talk to them about their hair and eye colour and the sort of clothes that they like to wear.

■ Be ready to prompt any children who find it difficult to ask for what they want.

■ Invite the children to cut out their completed figures and write their names on the back.

■ Look at the finished figures together and compare their clothes, hair and eye colour with those of the children that they represent.

■ Help younger children to cut out the figures.

■ Challenge older children to complete the back of their figure as well as the front.

More ideas

■ Encourage the children to play games such as 'Happy families' to practise asking others for things that they need.

■ Set up a baker's shop and encourage the 'shoppers' to ask for the items that they would like to buy.

Other curriculum areas

PD ■ Invite the children to play 'Skittles', 'Hoopla' and other turn-taking games with their friends.

MD ■ Play 'Shape snap' to encourage the children to speak up for themselves.

Home links
Ask parents and carers to let their children ask for tickets, goods or library books themselves.

Hey, that's mine!

Stepping Stone
Show confidence and the ability to stand up for own rights.

Early Learning Goal
Consider the consequences of their words and actions for themselves and others.

■

Group size
Up to four children.

■

What you need
A toy construction set; large soft doll or puppet.

What to do

■ Invite the children to play with a construction set.

■ Introduce the doll or puppet to the children and explain that it would like to play with them, but it is not very good at sharing or taking turns so it will need their help.

■ Ask the children to tell you if the doll does something wrong.

■ Manipulate the doll to play alongside the children, then after a few moments make it take something away from one of them.

■ If the child does not object, ask if they think the doll was correct to do what it did.

■ Talk about what the doll should have done and what it should do now.

■ Thank the children for their help and remind them to keep an eye on the doll in case it does anything else wrong.

■ Continue in this way, and every now and then, make the doll do something unsociable, each time discussing what has happened.

■ Younger children may become upset by the doll's bad behaviour, so ask an adult helper to be the victim.

■ Encourage older children to think about the consequences of various actions by asking questions such as 'What would happen if I punched someone if they did something wrong?' or 'What would happen if I burst into tears when something was taken off me?'.

More ideas

■ Invite visitors regularly into the group for the children to show around.

■ Ask a child to take over your role by calling the register, telling a story or organising snack-time.

Home links
Explain to parents and carers that you have been encouraging the children to think about the consequences of their own actions by asking 'What if...?' questions. Ask them to continue these discussions at home.

Other curriculum areas

KUW Take the children shopping or to the library and encourage them to do things for themselves.

CLL Provide a variety of different telephones, megaphones and microphones to encourage the children to speak confidently.

Personal, social and emotional development

I can catch

Stepping Stone
Have an awareness of the boundaries set and behavioural expectations within the setting.

Early Learning Goal
Consider the consequences of their words and actions for themselves and others.

■

Group size
Up to 12 children.

■

What you need
Four small balls; four large balls; four beanbags; four frisbees; large outdoor space; four different-coloured boxes; whistle or drum.

Home links
Explain to parents and carers that you have been emphasising the need for set boundaries and controlled behaviour by playing ball games. Encourage them to carry out similar activities at home with their children.

What to do
■ Put one of each item into the boxes and position them around the edge of the playing area.
■ Gather the children together and explain that you are going to play some throwing games.
■ Show the children the playing area and explain any necessary safety rules for your particular setting.
■ Tell the children that when you blow the whistle, they must stand very still holding their toy.
■ Invite three children to go to each of the boxes to choose something and try to remember which box it was from. Encourage them to play freely with the equipment.
■ After a few minutes blow the whistle and encourage the children to stand still.
■ Praise the children's sensible behaviour and remind them of the safety rules before inviting them to continue playing.
■ After a few more minutes, stop play again, this time inviting the children to replace their toy in the correct box and choose something different from another box.
■ Continue playing in this way for as long as the children remain focused and interested.
■ End the session by asking the children to line up in threes, holding the appropriate toys.
■ Place a box in front of each line of children and invite them to take turns to throw their toy into the box.
■ Support younger children by partnering them for a short while.
■ Encourage older children to join into groups of two or three and make up their own simple games to play.

More ideas
■ Play 'Musical statues' or 'Simon says' with the children.
■ Use beanbags to encourage the children to play simple relay games.

Other curriculum areas

CD Take paints, rollers and large cardboard boxes outside and invite the children to carry out some large-scale artwork. Talk about the need to be careful not to spill or splash any paint when they are painting.

MD Show the children how to use measuring equipment such as scales, callipers, rulers and tape measures.

Learning to become independent and self-reliant is an important part of growing up. Nurture this development by carrying out daily chores. Some of the activities in this chapter will give the children opportunities to set themselves challenges and share ideas.

What a mess!

What to do

■ Check for any skin allergies beforehand.

■ Gather the children and look at the dolls together.

■ Talk with the children about how the dolls might have got so dirty and ask them what they think should be done about it.

■ Invite each child to choose a doll or a set of clothes to wash, and help them to decide what they should use.

■ As they work, talk about their own washing or bath-time routines. Discuss the various items of equipment that they are using and why it is necessary to keep ourselves clean.

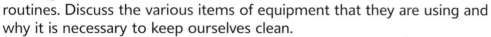

■ When the dolls are clean and towel-dried, discuss the need to leave them to drain for a while in case water has gone inside.

■ Once the clothes are clean, talk with the children about how and why they should be rinsed.

■ Discuss how the clothes will dry and help the children to peg them up on the washing line or on an airer.

■ Continue the activity with another group of children, if necessary, until everything is clean.

■ Work with just three or four younger children and help them to check that the clothes and dolls are clean.

■ Encourage older children to treat the dolls as though they were real people. Suggest that they do not hold them by the hair or get soap in their eyes!

More ideas

■ Provide dressing-up clothes that have a variety of fastenings for the children to practise.

■ Play games that involve removing and replacing shoes and socks.

Personal, social and emotional development

Goals for the Foundation Stage

Stepping Stone
Show willingness to tackle problems and enjoy self-chosen challenges.

Early Learning Goal
Dress and undress independently and manage their own personal hygiene.

■

Group size
Up to six children.

■

What you need
Washable, dressed dolls covered in mud, paint or jam; large bowls of warm water; sponges; soap; flannels; nail brushes; shampoo; towels; washing powder; washing line or airer; pegs.

Home links
Encourage parents and carers to provide shoes with easy fastenings, such as Velcro instead of laces, to encourage their children's independence.

Other curriculum areas

MD   Use sand-timers to challenge the children to put on and do up coats or shoes as quickly as possible.

CD   Ask the children to paint pictures to display over the wash basins to remind people to wash their hands.

Footprints

Demonstrate a sense of pride in own achievement.

Early Learning Goal
Dress and undress independently and manage their own personal hygiene.

■

Group size
Up to four children.

■

What you need
Trays of different-coloured paints; large sheets or long rolls of paper; chair; bowls of warm, soapy water; towels.

Home links
Ask parents and carers to encourage their children to put on their own coats and shoes.

PD **Other curriculum areas**
Sew a button on to one end of a short strip of material and cut a slit in the other to make a 'daisy'. Make several of these in different colours and let the children button them together to make 'daisy chains'.

MD Attach a strip of self-adhesive Velcro to a board. Use individual Velcro-backed number cards to make a number line to practise ordering.

What to do
■ Check for any skin allergies or foot infections.
■ Explain to the children that they are going to make footprint patterns on the paper.
■ Ask them to remove their shoes and socks or tights, and, if appropriate, roll up their trousers in preparation.
■ Invite a child to step into a tray of paint and walk on the paper to make a trail of footprints.
■ Place a chair and a bowl of warm soapy water nearby.
■ When the child has completed their trail, help them to step into the bowl of soapy water or sit down to wash their feet.
■ Invite another child to begin their trail.
■ Suggest that each child uses a different colour so the trails are easier to follow and will give interesting effects when two colours mix together.
■ Encourage and praise each child as they clean and dry their feet thoroughly and replace their footwear.
■ Remember to change the washing water for each child for hygiene reasons.
■ Display the finished prints for everyone to see.
■ Work with one younger child at a time in order to give all the necessary support.
■ Encourage older children to plan their trail first, and use different parts of their feet to make the prints.

More ideas
■ Provide dolls' clothes that have a variety of fastenings, for example, buckles, buttons, open-ended zips and so on.
■ Play 'Pass the clothes'. Invite the children to sit in a circle and pass around a basket of dressing-up clothes. When the music stops the child holding the basket should select an item, put it on and do it up.

Can you fasten it?

What to do
■ Gather the children together and look at the selection of clothes.

■ Talk about how each item of clothing is fastened and on which part of the body it is worn.

■ Tell the children that you would like them to find different pieces of clothing to put on and to fasten them without any help.

■ Invite each child to select an item of clothing and to put it on.

■ Once an item of clothing is on and fastened, invite the wearer to look in the mirror to check that it is fastened correctly and praise them enthusiastically before inviting them to find another piece.

■ If a child is struggling unduly, talk them through the procedure as you help them, congratulating them on what they have achieved.

■ Ensure that there are plenty of clothes with simple fastenings for younger children such as Velcro, closed-end zips, large buttons and so on.

■ Include complicated clothing for older children, for example, dungarees with buckled shoulder straps, tabards with side ties, all-in-one clown suits with press-stud fastenings and so on.

More ideas
■ Take photographs of various items of clothing and invite the children to put them into the correct sequence for getting dressed.

■ Dress a large doll or teddy incorrectly and ask the children to say what is wrong and to put it right.

Stepping Stone
Take initiatives and manage developmentally appropriate tasks.

■

Early Learning Goal
Dress and undress independently and manage their own personal hygiene.

■

Group size
Up to four children.

■

What you need
A selection of clothes with different fastenings such as press studs, zips, buckles, buttons, Velcro, laces and so on; full-length safety mirror.

Home links
Give each child a copy of the 'I can fasten' photocopiable sheet on page 92 to take home. Ask parents and carers to help their children practise the fastenings shown and to colour in the labels as they achieve them.

Other curriculum areas

PD Hold a clothes obstacle race. Space out a selection of clothes along the course and invite the children to race to the first item, put it on, do it up, then go on to the next item, until all the clothes have been collected. The winner is the person who gets back to the start wearing all their items of clothing correctly fastened.

KUW Provide a large doll and a selection of clothing and invite the children to dress it to suit the weather each day.

Polish and shine

Stepping Stone
Operate independently within the environment and show confidence in linking up with others for support and guidance.

Early Learning Goal
Dress and undress independently and manage their own personal hygiene.

Group size
Up to four children.

What you need
A selection of grubby leather shoes and boots; shoe cleaning materials; old shirts or coveralls; newspapers.

Home links
Explain to parents and carers that the children have been learning to polish shoes and ask them to let their children practise at home.

What to do
■ Talk to the children about keeping shoes and boots clean. Remind them that they must not do any polishing or cleaning at home without an adult's permission and help.
■ Look at the selection of footwear and talk about how untidy they look. What do the children think needs to be done?
■ Talk about how the shoes and boots should be cleaned. Do the children think that they should be washed or polished?

■ Ensure that all the children are well protected by a back-to-front old shirt or coverall, and that surfaces are covered in old newspapers.
■ Demonstrate how to apply polish and buff it to a shine.
■ Invite the children to polish the shoes and boots.
■ Observe and help the children as they work, talking about how the polish will protect the footwear and make it last longer as well as look better.
■ When the shoes are polished to the children's satisfaction, help them to examine them carefully to make sure that all parts are clean and not just the toe cap.
■ Once all the shoes have been cleaned, invite the children to wash their hands thoroughly using soap and water and a nail brush, if necessary.
■ Stress the importance of drying hands carefully, especially between the fingers, to prevent them from getting sore.
■ Work with two younger children at a time and use polish applicators instead of tins of polish.
■ Have a range of different cleaning materials available, for example, coloured as well as clear or neutral creams, brushes, sponges and cloths. Help older children to decide which are the most appropriate for the shoes or boots that they are cleaning.

More ideas
■ Collect together some brassware, silverware and coins and have a metal-polishing session, or provide buckets and sponges and wash low-level windows.
■ Encourage the children to use a sweeper to clean up their own dry messes.

Other curriculum areas
CLL Read *Mr Messy* by Roger Hargreaves (Egmont Books) and talk with the children about all the things that he did wrong.

KUW Provide a giant set of teeth and a big brush for the children to practise cleaning teeth.

Personal, social and emotional development

Rainy-day fun

What to do

■ Tell the children that you are going to go outside and explore some puddles and other wet things.

■ Invite them to go outside briefly to see whether the rain is heavy or light, and whether it is warm, cold or windy. Then ask the children what sort of clothes they think they should wear.

■ When the children have decided what the weather is, encourage them to get themselves ready with as little help as possible.

■ Go outside and look in puddles and talk about what you see. What happens if you blow the surface of the water?

■ Talk about whether the children are wearing suitable footwear to step in the puddles.

■ Find leaves and sticks to float in the deeper puddles and talk about why the puddles are where they are.

■ Look at other wet things and notice drips, dribbles and streams of water forming in different places, and listen to the sounds that the rain makes on different surfaces.

■ Invite the children to turn their faces up to the rain and talk about how it feels.

■ Encourage the children to look at their clothing and notice its wetness, how it feels and what it looks like. Invite them to talk about what they should do with it when they go indoors.

■ Return indoors, reminding the children to remove their wellingtons, and encourage them to take off their own coats and hang them to dry.

■ Provide towels for the children to dry their wet faces and hands.

■ If necessary, help younger children to take off their wellingtons.

■ Encourage older children to draw pictures to show what they did outside in the rain.

More ideas

■ Chalk pictures on the ground outside on a dry day and use a watering can to see what happens to them when it rains.

■ Encourage the children to play outdoors whatever the weather and to think carefully each time about what they should wear.

Other curriculum areas

CLL Make a collection of rainy-day words to hang on 'raindrops' from the ceiling.

KUW Look at the different items of clothing to find their suitability for wearing in the rain or in the cold.

Personal, social and emotional development

Hmm! I wonder...

What to do
■ Let the children explore and play freely with the selection of cardboard boxes and tubes.

■ When the children have gone beyond the inevitable 'build it high and knock it down' stage, gather them together and talk about what sort of things they could construct using the boxes.

■ If you are working on a particular theme, link the ideas to this, for example, ambulances and fire engines for Transport, or castles and houses for Buildings.

■ Give the children several options and ask them to think about which they would like to try to build.

■ Suggest that the children might like to use the pencils and paper to draw pictures to help them decide what to build.

■ Allow plenty of time for the construction work and be ready to help with practical suggestions if necessary.

■ Talk to the children as they work and encourage them to explain what they are doing.

■ When they have completed their creations, let the children play with them bringing the session to a close.

■ It may be necessary to have several free-play sessions over a period of time to familiarise younger children with the boxes before they are ready to complete a specific challenge.

■ Encourage older children to examine their finished creation carefully, then ask them to say how they think it could be modified to make it even better.

More ideas
■ Challenge the children to build the tallest tower or the longest tunnel in the sand tray and encourage them to think of challenges to set each other.

■ Provide a selection of resources in the water tray and challenge the children to make the heavy objects float and the light objects sink.

Other curriculum areas
MD Copy the 'Tangram pattern' photocopiable sheet on page 93 on to different-coloured sheets of card and cut out the tangrams. Give each child a set and challenge them to make a boat or a house.

CD Provide a selection of recyclable materials and place three different-sized bears nearby. Challenge the children to make a chair or bed for one of the bears.

Personal, social and emotional development

Fabulous fish

What to do

◼ Look at the pictures of the fish with the children and talk about the shapes and colours of them.

◼ Tell the children that you would like to turn the wall into an underwater scene.

◼ Mix some watery, pale blue paint and demonstrate how to sponge-paint waves across the paper.

◼ Let the children take turns to make waves. Then repeat with watery dark blue paint until everyone has had a turn.

◼ Give each child a piece of card and ask them to draw a large fish shape, then cut it out. Encourage them to decorate it using the collage materials.

◼ Suggest that the children make other items for the collage, such as seaweed, shells, anemones and so on, referring to the pictures if necessary.

◼ When everything is dry, invite the children to attach the items into position on the wall with Blu-Tack.

◼ Talk about the scene as it develops, helping the children to modify it as they go along.

◼ Dangle any excess items from the ceiling to hang in front of the picture to give a 3-D effect.

◼ When the children are happy with the underwater scene, paste the items into position and invite them to bring a friend to admire the work.

◼ Provide younger children with pre-cut fish shapes to ensure a good variety of size, shape and direction.

◼ Encourage older children to name their fish, using their colour, pattern and habitat as inspiration, for example, the red-spotted rock fish.

More ideas

◼ Make paper flowers and place them in vases to decorate your book corner.

◼ Have a gallery to display the children's best pieces of work, updating it regularly.

Stepping Stone
Demonstrate a sense of pride in own achievement.

Early Learning Goal
Select and use activities and resources independently.

◼

Group size
Up to eight children.

◼

What you need
Pictures of colourful tropical fish and underwater scenes; display wall at child-height covered in neutral backing paper; wide range of craft and collage materials; paint; sponges; paper; card; scissors; Blu-Tack or similar; glue.

Home links
Let the children hear you praising their achievements to their parents and carers.

Other curriculum areas

PD Provide a range of small outdoor equipment such as safety darts, plastic golf clubs, bats, balls, quoits, hoops and so on. Encourage the children to demonstrate their developing physical skills to you.

CD Set up a music corner with song books, instruments and a tape recorder. Invite the children to record their singing and music, and play it to the group at the end of a session.

Personal, social and emotional development

It's a masterpiece!

Stepping Stone
Take initiatives and manage developmentally appropriate tasks.

Early Learning Goal
Select and use activities and resources independently.
■
Group size
Up to four children.
■
What you need
Large table; aprons; paint; mixing palettes and trays; paintbrushes; paint rollers; sponges; rags; large sheet of paper.

Home links
Invite parents and carers to come in to teach the children skills such as plaiting, weaving or sewing.

What to do
■ Spread out the large sheet of paper on a large table and arrange the painting materials close by.
■ Ensure that the children are well protected by aprons before inviting them to select a paint roller, paintbrush, sponge or rag and some paint.
■ Explain to the children that they can paint whatever they would like to, and help them to decide whether they will work together on one large picture or each have a section of the paper to paint.
■ Encourage each child to use a variety of equipment and to experiment using it in different ways, for example, the edge of the roller will produce a finer line, sponges can be patted or wiped across the paper and so on.
■ Invite the children to use the palettes to mix their own colours and to share ideas with each other.
■ Continue painting until the children decide that the masterpiece is completely finished!
■ Look at the work together and talk about its colour and form before leaving it to dry.
■ Invite the children to suggest what should happen to the painting now. Should it be displayed in the setting, cut into pieces and shared between them, thrown away or taken home by one person?
■ Younger children may need help to mix colours to avoid everything turning muddy brown.
■ Encourage older children to make simple plans before they begin painting.

Other curriculum areas
CLL Provide paper, writing materials, a hole-punch, ribbon, sticky tape and small stapler and challenge the children to make a book about themselves.
MD Provide standard measuring equipment, ribbon, string and sets of non-standard but regular-sized objects, such as wooden cubes, cereal boxes and strips of card, and ask the children to find different ways of measuring themselves.

More ideas
■ Provide tiny sheets of paper, paint, small twigs, feathers and cotton buds to produce miniature paintings.
■ Invite individual children to choose circle-time games that they would like to play or perhaps lead.

Personal, social and emotional development

Look what I've made!

What to do

■ Tell the children that you have only one piece of play dough. Explain that you would like everyone to have a piece and you do not know what to do. Wait for the children to decide upon a course of action – which will hopefully involve sharing out the dough!

■ Invite a child to divide up the dough between the children.

■ Then tell the children that you would also like to play with the dough and let them decide how to solve that problem.

■ Sit alongside the children, talking to them as they work and asking their advice about how to make different things such as a snail, a flower or a banana.

■ Encourage the children to demonstrate the different techniques that they are using and to show you how to get different effects with the mark-making tools.

■ Remember to model appropriate social behaviour throughout the activity, ensuring that your talk often includes 'please', 'thank you' and 'excuse me'.

■ Pause the activity occasionally with younger children to clear up any dough that has been dropped on the floor and talk about why it is necessary to do this.

■ Challenge older children to make objects belonging to a particular set, for example, crockery, fruit, animals or clothing.

More ideas

■ Store the role-play equipment in different boxes and let the children decide which ones to use during a particular session.

■ Provide bubble liquid and Connecta Straws in the water tray and encourage the children to make frameworks, such as cubes or pyramids, to dip into the liquid to create different-shaped bubbles.

Other curriculum areas

CD Decide on a favourite story to act out and then help the children to design and make appropriate props to use for different characters.

KUW Go for a walk around your local area, letting the children decide which way to go. Encourage them to draw a map of the route when they return to the setting.

Stepping Stone
Take initiatives and manage developmentally appropriate tasks.

Early Learning Goal
Select and use activities and resources independently.

■

Group size
Up to four children.

■

What you need
Play dough (see the recipe on the 'Play-dough recipe' photocopiable sheet on page 94); selection of cutters, rolling pins and mark-making tools.

Home links
Invite each child to bring something from home to show to their friends and say why they chose it.

Personal, social and emotional development

I'm hungry

Early Learning Goal
Select and use activities resources independently.

Group size
Up to four children at a time.

What you need
Different sorts of bread; low-fat spread; variety of sandwich fillings; knives; plates; aprons; cling film or tin foil; paper; pencils; cocktail sticks.

What to do
- Check for any food allergies and dietary requirements.
- Ensure that the children's hands and the work surfaces are thoroughly clean before you start.
- Invite the children to work in pairs to decide which type of bread they would like to use to make a sandwich, how to prepare it and what to put inside it.
- Help the children to decide whether their chosen filling needs preparing in any way or whether it can be used as it is.

- When the children have made their sandwiches, talk about the size of them and invite each pair to decide whether to cut them smaller or leave them as they are.
- Ask the children to arrange their finished sandwiches on a plate, then add an identifying label, for example, 'Cheese and tomato by Abigail and Zak'. Cover the sandwiches with cling film and put them to one side until they are needed.
- Repeat the activity with further groups until there are enough sandwiches for everyone.
- At snack time, invite the chefs to hand round their plates of sandwiches to the other children.
- Slice any items, such as tomatoes or cucumber, for younger children.
- Encourage older children to make their own labels.

More ideas
- Play simple team relay games that rely on co-operation between team members.
- Enlist pairs of volunteers to do jobs such as emptying the water tray or sweeping up the sand.

Home links
Explain to parents and carers that you have been encouraging the children to work together to complete various tasks and ask them to continue at home.

Other curriculum areas
CLL Invite a pair of children to tell the group a favourite story or recite a rhyme.

PD Play 'Hot potato' in which everyone must stand still until they are given a 'hot potato' (beanbag). Then they must run quickly to give it to someone else before it burns their fingers. Use four or five beanbags for a group of 20 children.

Children attending your setting will have come from a variety of backgrounds. Celebrate this diversity by providing opportunities for them to gain an understanding of different customs and cultures and to express feelings about their own lives with these ideas.

Jelly good fun!

What to do

■ Ensure that all the surfaces, equipment and the children's hands are thoroughly clean.

■ Check for any food allergies or dietary requirements.

■ Give each child a bowl, a spoon and three or four cubes of jelly.

■ Warn the children that the water is very hot and could burn them, so they must stand well back as you pour 50ml of hot water into their bowls.

■ Invite the children to stir the jelly until the cubes dissolve.

■ As the children work, talk about why they are making the jellies (to share with friends at a small party) and encourage the children to tell you about any parties that they have been to and the sort of food that they ate there.

■ When the jelly has completely dissolved, make up each bowl to the required amount using cold water. (Shorten the setting time by using ice cubes instead of cold water and stirring until they dissolve.)

■ Repeat the activity with other children until you have sufficient jelly for the whole group.

■ While the jellies are setting, arrange a party area and invite a group of children to set out a teaspoon and small dish for each child in the group, talking about family parties as they do so.

■ When the jellies are ready to eat, invite some of the children to act as servers and help them to place a large spoonful of jelly in everyone's dish.

■ Make the party more intimate for younger children by letting them invite a friend each.

■ Encourage older children to make invitations for the group to attend the party.

More ideas

■ Create a news corner where the children can display pictures of things that they have done at home.

■ Take the children on a shopping trip and encourage them to talk about personal shopping experiences elsewhere.

Personal, social and emotional development

Goals for the Foundation Stage

Stepping Stone
Make connections between different parts of their life experience.

Early Learning Goal
Understand that people have different needs, views, cultures and beliefs, that need to be treated with respect.

Group size
Four children.

What you need
Two packets of jelly; a bowl and stirring spoon for each child; measuring jug; hot water (adult use); cold water or ice cubes; a small dish and teaspoon for each child.

Home links
Ask parents and carers to let their children bring in family photographs of parties to share with the group.

Other curriculum areas

MD Make a pictogram to show the children's favourite party foods.

KUW Ask the children to compare your setting with their homes, for example, the size of furniture and fittings, layout, colour schemes and so on.

Happy Eid

Stepping Stone
Show a strong sense of self as a member of different communities, such as their family or setting.

Early Learning Goal
Understand that people have different needs, views, cultures and beliefs, that need to be treated with respect.

Group size
Four children.

What you need
Black or dark blue A4 card; glue; scissors; yellow, white, silver or gold paper; pens; pencils; commercial Eid cards.

Home links
Let the children take the Eid cards home for their families to enjoy. If appropriate, also send an accompanying note explaining about the festival.

What to do
■ Invite the children to choose black or dark blue card. Help them to fold it in half to make a greetings card, then to place it in front of them so that the fold is on the right-hand side.

■ Encourage the children to choose a caption to write on the inside of their card, for example, 'Happy Eid' or 'Eid Mubarak' and 'Love from ...' and help them to write it.

■ Talk about the festival of Eid-ul-Fitre. Invite those children of the Muslim faith to explain it to others who may know little about its significance.

■ Encourage listeners to ask questions and help the speakers to answer them. If any questions are asked to which you do not know the answer, tell the children that you will try to find out (and remember to do so!).

■ Then invite each child to select some white, yellow, gold or silver paper to make a moon and star to add to their Eid card.

■ Help the children to draw and cut out a thin crescent moon and a five-pointed star and paste them on to the front of their card.

■ Cut out moons and stars for younger children.

■ Show older children the commercial Eid cards to inspire them to create a design of their own from the materials that are available.

More ideas
■ Encourage the children to bring in any medals, badges or certificates that they may have been awarded at a local group or club. Invite them to explain a little about the club to the rest of the group, saying how and why they received the award.

■ Create a portrait gallery for the children to display pictures of their family members.

Other curriculum areas

KUW Provide a variety of dressing-up clothes from around the world, including lengths of coloured materials that the children can use as saris, sarongs and so on.

CLL Invite the children to record a short description of their home and family on to a tape, play it back and talk about any similarities and differences that they notice between the different families.

Christingle

What to do

■ Give each child an orange and tell them that they are going to make a Christingle.

■ Explain that Christingle means Christ Light and the orange represents the world.

■ Help each child to fix a length of ribbon around the middle of their orange and explain that this signifies Jesus' death and resurrection.

■ Give each child four cocktail sticks and tell them that they represent spring, summer, autumn and winter.

■ Place the fruit and sweets in the centre of the table and explain to the children that these represent the earth's produce.

■ Invite the children to skewer a selection of fruit and sweets on to their sticks and insert them around the circumference of their orange.

■ As the children work, talk about the produce of the world and how some countries are so poor that they do not have enough food for all the people that live there. Remind the children how lucky we are in this country to be able to eat what we want, when we want to.

■ Finally, help each child to place a candle in the top of their orange and explain that this represents Jesus bringing light into the world.

■ Emphasise that candles are very dangerous and that the children should never light them.

■ Make stands from cardboard tubes for younger children to rest their Christingles on.

■ Encourage older children to make and decorate their own Christingle stands.

More ideas

■ Invite storytellers in to tell the children stories from different countries.

■ Provide a variety of dual-language books containing stories from different cultures.

Other curriculum areas

CD Invite the children to make diva lamps from clay to celebrate Divali.

PD Learn some simple dance steps from different cultures such as the Irish jig, flamenco dancing and the hula.

Personal, social and emotional development

How are you today?

Stepping Stone
Have a positive self-image and show that they are comfortable with themselves.

Early Learning Goal
Understand that people have different needs, views, cultures and beliefs, that need to be treated with respect.

Group size
Whole group.

What you need
To be familiar with the song 'If You're Happy and You Know It, Clap Your Hands' from *This Little Puffin...* compiled by Elizabeth Matterson (Puffin Books).

Home links
Ask parents and carers to write a short sentence praising their child, for example, 'I am proud of Nadhir because he can dress himself' and to encourage their child to illustrate it for a 'Proud parents' display.

What to do
■ Sing the song with the children, encouraging all of them to join in with the actions.

■ Tell the children that you are going to sing another verse and although you know the words you are not sure what actions to do.

■ Explain that you are going to be sad this time and ask for suggestions for actions, for example, wipe your eyes, cuddle a teddy and so on.

■ Sing the verse using the chosen actions and talk about being sad, then invite them to think of a mood for the next verse, such as cross, frightened, worried and so on, and invent actions to go with the mood.

■ Finish on a positive note by repeating the first verse.

■ Be ready to support younger children who may become upset when they recall past experiences that caused them fear or worry.

■ With older children sing 'If she's (sad) and she knows it...' and encourage them to think of ways to alleviate the various moods of a third person.

More ideas
■ Make a 'We can...' board by choosing a different skill each week, for example, 'We can hop', 'We can count to five', 'We can find blue things' and so on. Add the children's names to the 'We can...' board every day to celebrate their various achievements.

■ Make a point of giving a reward sticker to the children for any positive behaviour that you notice such as picking up a fallen book instead of stepping over it, helping a distressed child and so on. Explain to the group the reason for awarding it so as to encourage the other children to follow suit.

Other curriculum areas
CLL Adapt a puppet theatre to resemble a television and encourage the children to practise speaking to an audience as a newscaster, weather forecaster or programme presenter.

MD Play a game of 'Five' and invite the children to take turns to come to the front to pick out five other children who must then say something positive about them.

I like this one

What to do

■ Look at the posters, photographs and picture books together. Encourage the children to ask questions and talk about what they see.

■ Point out similarities as well as differences between the various items of clothing shown and compare them with what the children are wearing.

■ Introduce the dressing-up clothes and encourage the children to find items to match those in the books and photographs.

■ Talk about who is wearing the different items and encourage the children to say what they like and dislike about the various costumes.

■ Explain to the children that there are not enough clothes for everyone to wear them at the same time, so they will have to take turns to dress up in them.

■ Invite six or eight children to try on the clothes while the rest of the group carry out other activities.

■ Finish by inviting a child to choose a story for you to read and discuss with the whole group.

■ Younger children may need considerable help to tie a sarong or wrap a turban.

■ Encourage older children to draw a picture of themselves wearing their favourite costume.

More ideas

■ Visit and compare different places of worship each month.

■ Invite different religious leaders in to show the children some relevant artefacts and explain a little about them.

Other curriculum areas

CD Provide a selection of multicultural instruments to give the activity an added dimension.

MD Set up a role-play shop selling saris for the children to practise measuring and using money.

Stepping Stone
Have an awareness of, and show interest and enjoyment in, cultural and religious differences.

Early Learning Goal
Understand that people have different needs, views, cultures and beliefs, that need to be treated with respect.

Group size
Whole group introduction; six to eight children.

What you need
Dressing-up clothes and accessories from around the world, for example, saris, shalwal-kameez, djellabas, sarongs, hats and so on; posters, photographs and picture books showing multicultural costumes being worn by adults and children in their country of origin; full-length safety mirrors; dual-language story-books from other countries; drawing and writing materials.

Home links
Invite parents and carers to help make more costumes to build up your collection of dressing-up clothes.

Personal, social and emotional development

That's delicious!

Early Learning Goal
Understand that they can expect others to treat their needs, views, cultures and beliefs with respect.

Group size
Whole group.

What you need
A selection of fresh and processed food from different countries; knives; paper plates; atlas or globe; card; pens.

Home links
Ask parents and carers to give the children a cookery demonstration of a favourite recipe from another country.

What to do
■ Check for any food allergies or dietary requirements.
■ Prepare each food item into small pieces for the children to taste, leaving some whole so that they can see what it looked like.
■ Make identification labels for each food item.
■ Gather the children together and explain that you have lots of different foods that have all come from different countries for them to taste.
■ Look at the first food item together.
■ Talk about what sort of food it is, for example, fruit, vegetable, bread, and discuss which country it originates from.
■ Point out the position of the country in relation to the British Isles on a globe or in an atlas.
■ Pass the pieces of food around for the group to touch, smell, taste and talk about.
■ Put each food to one side with its identification label nearby.
■ Younger children may be reluctant to try unfamiliar food so encourage them to look at it and smell it, then ask them to tell you if they later change their mind about tasting it.
■ Encourage older children to find some of the countries of origin on a globe or in an atlas.

Other curriculum areas
KUW Introduce a 'Travelling Ted' to be taken on holiday by the children. Ask them to take photographs of him in different places and to fill in his diary to help the rest of the group learn about different places in this country and abroad.
CLL Learn to say 'hello' and 'goodbye' in other languages.

More ideas
■ Find out about different forms of transport from around the world.
■ Look in books at houses and homes in different parts of the world.

Personal, social and emotional development

This little light of mine

candles are used for birthdays

What to do
■ Gather the children together and talk to them about light and its various sources, including the sun.
■ Encourage the children to think and talk about how they might feel if the world was in permanent darkness.
■ Explain that, a long time ago, people had only fires to lighten their darkness. Then candles were invented.
■ Tell the children that candles are important in many different religions, for many different reasons, for example, at Divali, during Advent and Hanukkah and the festival of St Lucia.
■ Invite the children to tell you about any times that they and their families use candles, and ask them to tell everyone something about what the candles represent.
■ Show the children the selection of materials and explain that they are going to take turns to make and decorate a model candle of their own.
■ Talk to the small group of children about the use and significance of candles as they paint or decorate their tube. Invite them to add a tissue-paper flame to complete their candle.
■ Display the children's finished candles alongside informative labels explaining how candles are used in various festivals and cultural events.
■ Help younger children by holding their tube still as they decorate it.
■ Challenge older children to try to decorate their candles with a repeating pattern.

More ideas
■ Use the model candles to hold a candlelit 'multi-faith service' arranged by the children.
■ Visit different places of worship to see how candles are used.

Other curriculum areas
PD Practise a few simple yoga exercises.

CLL Encourage the children to write their name (or initials) in a different script.

Stepping Stone
Show a strong sense of self as a member of different communities, such as their family or setting.

Early Learning Goal
Understand that they can expect others to treat their needs, views, cultures and beliefs with respect.

Group size
Whole group introduction, then four to six children.

What you need
Kitchen-roll tubes; art and craft materials; picture books and posters showing candles inside various places of worship and during processions and festivals.

Home links
Ask the children to bring in photographs of their christening, baptism or naming ceremony to share with the rest of the group.

Personal, social and emotional development

The dreidel game

Early Learning Goal
Understand that they can expect others to treat their needs, views, cultures and beliefs with respect.

Group size
Up to six children.

What you need
The 'Dreidel cube' photocopiable sheet on page 95; pencil; counters.

Preparation
Copy the photocopiable sheet on to thin card, cut along the solid outline and fold along the dotted lines to make the cube, gluing the flaps to secure. Create a hole through the top and bottom of the cube and push a pencil through. Twirl the pencil to spin the dreidel.

What to do
■ Explain to the children that the dreidel is a traditional Jewish game that is often played during the festival of Hanukkah.
■ Talk about other games that the children in the group play at home with their families.
■ Look at the cube and talk about the words and symbols shown. Explain that each one means something different: 'nun' means nothing; 'gimel' means everything; 'shin' means give and 'hey' means take.
■ Give each child ten counters and put the same amount in the centre of the table.
■ Explain the rules of the game to the children.
■ Highlight each face of the cube with a different colour for younger children to help them recognise the different words and symbols.
■ Encourage older children to use the Hebrew words shown on the cube as they play the game.

More ideas
■ Continue celebrating Hanukkah by trying some Jewish food such as latkes (potato pancakes) or sufganyot (doughnuts).
■ Celebrate a variety of festivals from different cultures and religions throughout the year.

Home links
Give each child a copy of the photocopiable sheet to take home so that they can play the game with their parents and carers.

Other curriculum areas
CLL Let the children practise writing the dreidel names and symbols.
KUW Explore the Internet for games from other cultures and religions.

Personal, social and emotional development

I feel happy

What to do

■ Remind the children of the variations on the song that you sang in the 'How are you today?' activity. Ask them if they can remember some of the actions.

■ Call out a mood or feeling and ask the children to mime it. Do this several times to make sure that they all understand what a mime is.

■ Invite a child to come to the front of the group to do a mime for everyone to guess.

■ Ask the child to pick a mood card without letting

the rest of the group see it. Does the child know what the mood is? (If they are unsure, have a whispered consultation out of earshot of the group before the mime begins.)

■ When a child guesses the mimed mood correctly, ask the mime artist to explain why the person on the card might be in that particular mood.

■ Ask the whole group to consider whether it is a positive mood that should be encouraged or a negative one that needs to be improved.

■ Talk with the children about how everyone can help themselves to get over a negative mood.

■ Invite another child to do a mime and repeat the process.

■ Suggest that younger children mime with a friend if they do not feel confident enough to do it alone.

■ Encourage older children to devise a strategy to use to prevent an outburst if they feel that they are about to get unduly angry.

More ideas

■ Listen to various types of music, for example, classical, popular, loud, soft, slow, fast and so on. Encourage the children to tell you how it makes them feel.

■ Sit in a circle and pass round a microphone. Invite everyone to say a few words about themselves.

Other curriculum areas

CD Invite the children to paint pictures of faces showing different emotions. Place mirrors nearby so that they can see what their own happy, angry or sad face looks like.

PD Let the children practise moving around the room in different moods.

Stepping Stone
Have a positive self-image and show that they are comfortable with themselves.

Early Learning Goal
Understand that they can expect others to treat their needs, views, cultures and beliefs with respect.

Group size
Whole group.

What you need
Experience of the activity 'How are you today?' on page 72; the 'How do you feel?' photocopiable sheet on page 96.

Preparation
Copy the photocopiable sheet on to card, colour, cut out and laminate to make a set of mood cards.

Home links
Ask parents and carers to help their children collect pictures from old newspapers and magazines showing people displaying different emotions.

Let's get married

Stepping Stone
Have an awareness of, and show interest and enjoyment in, cultural and religious differences.

Early Learning Goal
Understand that they can expect others to treat their needs, views, cultures and beliefs with respect.

Group size
Whole group introduction, then six to eight children.

What you need
Information about wedding ceremonies performed by different ethnic and religious groups; suitable props and dressing-up clothes relevant to one ceremony of your choice; cameras.

What to do

■ Talk to the whole group about why and where people get married.
■ Invite the children to take turns to tell the group about any weddings that they have attended. Ask if they have ever been a bridesmaid or a page boy.
■ Explain that there are many different ways to get married, but you are just going to talk about one in particular.
■ Look at the props and clothing and talk about what each is for and how it is used.
■ Invite a small group of children to take turns to dress up.
■ Talk to them about such things as the special clothes that the bride and groom wear and the seating arrangements of friends and relatives.

■ Discuss the ceremony itself and the significance of things such as the rings.
■ Explain what happens after the ceremony, for example, people have something to eat, speeches are made, goodwill messages are received and people dance.
■ Concentrate mostly on the clothes and props rather than the details of the ceremony with younger children.
■ Encourage older children to plan an order of events for a wedding day and try to follow it.

More ideas

■ Cut out pictures from old travel brochures and make a collage of life in a particular country.
■ Listen to songs in different languages. Encourage the children to say what they like about them, even though they may not be able to understand the words.

Other curriculum areas

PD Have fun trying to use chopsticks.

MD Encourage the children to learn to count to five in several different languages.

PSED (1)

Name _____

Goals	Assessment	Date
Dispositions and attitudes		
Continue to be interested, excited and motivated to learn		
Be confident to try new activities, initiate ideas and speak in a familiar group		
Maintain attention, concentrate, and sit quietly when appropriate		
Self-confidence and self-esteem		
Respond to significant experiences, showing a range of feelings when appropriate		
Have a developing awareness of their own needs, views and feelings and be sensitive to the needs, views and feelings of others		
Have a developing respect for their own cultures and beliefs and those of other people		

PSED (2)

Name _____

Goals	Assessment	Date
Making relationships Form good relationships with adults and peers		
Work as part of a group or class, taking turns and sharing fairly, understanding that there needs to be agreed values and codes of behaviour for groups of people, including adults and children, to work together harmoniously		
Behaviour and self-control Understand what is right, what is wrong, and why		
Consider the consequences of their words and actions for themselves and others		

PSED (3)

Name _____

Goals	Assessment	Date
Self-care		
Dress and undress independently and manage their own personal hygiene		
Select and use resources independently		
Sense of community		
Understand that people have different needs, views, cultures and beliefs, that need to be treated with respect		
Understand that they can expect others to treat their needs, views, cultures and beliefs with respect		

Observation record sheet

Activity: Date:

Child/children: Observer:

Focus of observation:

Time	Name	What child is doing/saying	Evaluation/support extension

Comments:

Photocopiable   **Personal, social and emotional development**

Dice bingo

1		5	
	6		3
4			
	2		
1		5	
	6		3
4			
	2		

Tell a story

Photocopiable

Personal, social and emotional development

Our day

activity time

snack time

story time

Here are the three bears. They live in a house in the wild, wild wood.

circle time

home time

Oh dear!

Photocopiable

Personal, social and emotional development

Find your other half (page 40)

Farmyard friends

Personal, social and emotional development   **Photocopiable**

Lost and found!

What you need
A dice; counter for each player.

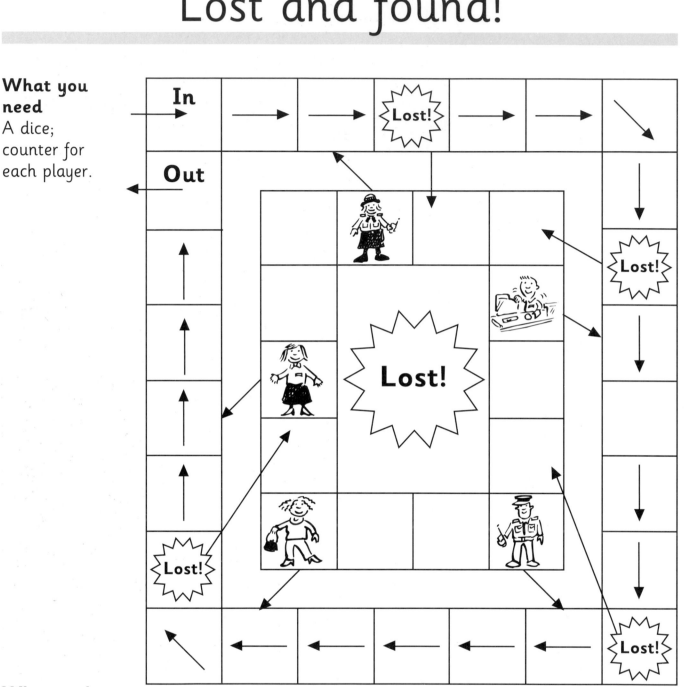

What to do

1 Take turns to roll the dice and enter the shopping centre on the appropriate square.

2 If a player lands on a Lost! square they should move on to the inner track as shown by the arrow and go round that track until they land on a suitable person to escort them back to the shopping area (outer track).

3 With each roll of the dice, lost players can choose which direction to move on the inner track to enable them to find help as soon as possible.

4 When they find a suitable person they can move back on to the outer track as indicated.

5 The first player to leave the shopping centre safely is the winner.

Photocopiable   **Personal, social and emotional development**

Litter pick

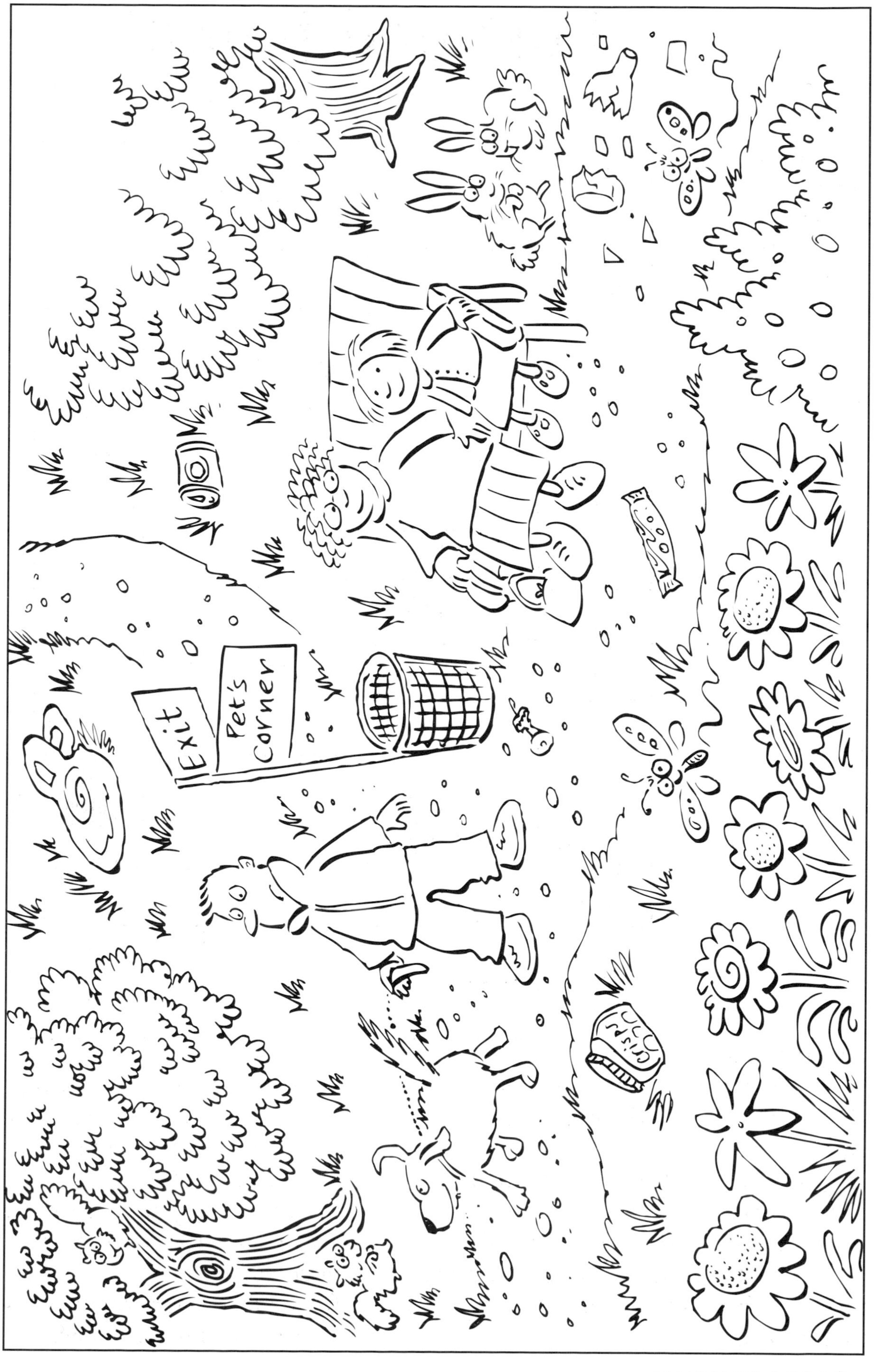

Exit

Pet's Corner

Learning partnership

Within this setting we will endeavour to:
- encourage your child to do their best at all times
- create a safe yet stimulating environment to promote effective learning
- encourage the children to care for their surroundings and have respect for others they meet
- offer a broad range of activities and experiences in line with the Foundation Stage curriculum
- keep parents and carers and regularly informed of their child's progress.

To support this partnership we expect parents to:
- make sure their child arrives on time and is collected promptly at the end of the session
- support the setting in upholding high standards of behaviour
- keep us fully informed of any difficulties or problems that their child may be experiencing.

We also expect the children to:
- take good care of equipment, books and the environment
- be friendly, helpful, polite and courteous towards others
- have a positive attitude towards new experiences and learning
- be truthful and show respect towards the needs of others.

Photocopiable

Personal, social and emotional development

This is me

I can fasten

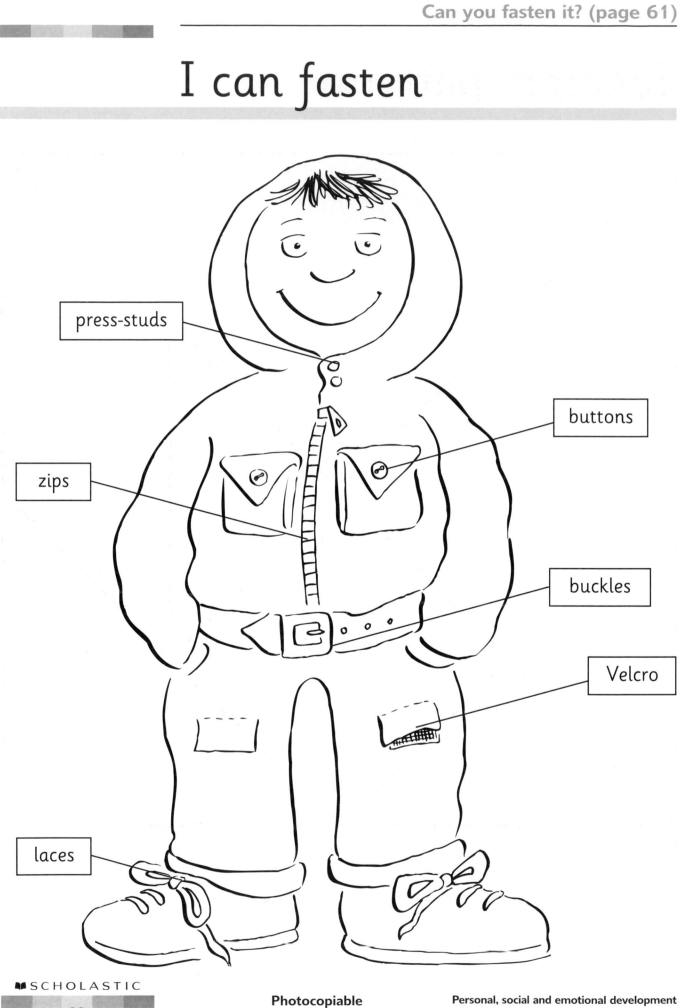

press-studs

buttons

zips

buckles

Velcro

laces

Photocopiable

Personal, social and emotional development

Tangram pattern

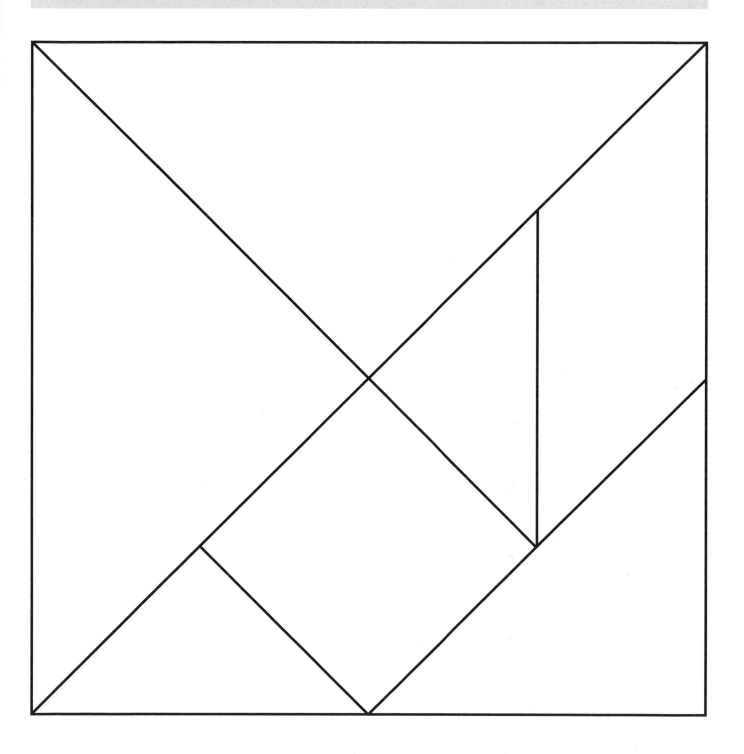

Play-dough recipe

Ingredients

2 cups plain flour
2 cups water
1 cup salt
1 tablespoon cooking oil

2 teaspoons cream
of tartar
food colouring

This play dough is soft and pliable and will keep fresh for several weeks if stored in a plastic bag in a refrigerator between uses. If left exposed to the air it will harden and can then be painted or varnished for a lasting finish.

What to do

1 Put all ingredients into a large saucepan on a gentle heat.

2 Stir continuously until mixture leaves the side of the pan.

3 Leave to cool.

4 Roll into a ball and store in a plastic bag or sealed container in a refrigerator or cool place.

Photocopiable

Personal, social and emotional development

Dreidel cube

Cut along the solid lines, fold along the dotted lines and glue the flaps to secure. Push a pencil through the two circles on the cube.

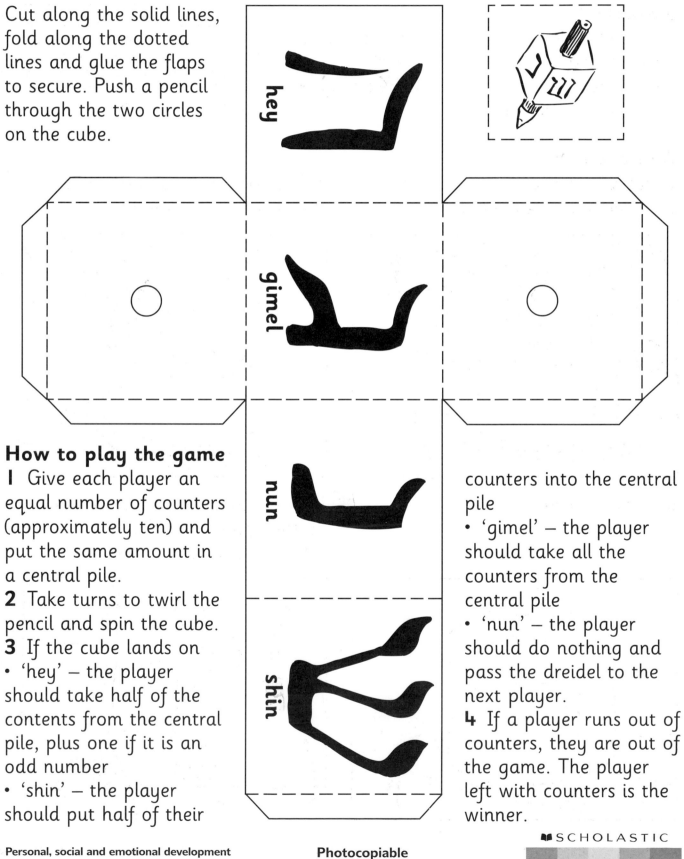

hey

gimel

nun

shin

How to play the game

1 Give each player an equal number of counters (approximately ten) and put the same amount in a central pile.

2 Take turns to twirl the pencil and spin the cube.

3 If the cube lands on

• 'hey' – the player should take half of the contents from the central pile, plus one if it is an odd number

• 'shin' – the player should put half of their counters into the central pile

• 'gimel' – the player should take all the counters from the central pile

• 'nun' – the player should do nothing and pass the dreidel to the next player.

4 If a player runs out of counters, they are out of the game. The player left with counters is the winner.

How do you feel?

Photocopiable

Personal, social and emotional development